It's In To Be Thin...

The Diet Workshop Way

by Lois Lyons Lindauer

PRENTICE-HALL, INC.

Englewood Cliffs, N. J.

*This book is dedicated to the proposition
that all men, women and children are
created with an equal right to be thin.*

Second printing............August, 1971

IT'S IN TO BE THIN... THE DIET WORKSHOP WAY
by Lois Lyons Lindauer

© 1970 by Universal Publishing and Distributing Corporation

Library of Congress Catalog Card Number: 71-112970

Printed in the United States of America · *T*
ISBN 0-13-506576-3

Prentice-Hall International, Inc., London
Prentice-Hall of Australia, Pty. Ltd., Sydney
Prentice-Hall of Canada, Ltd., Toronto
Prentice-Hall of India Private Ltd., New Delhi
Prentice-Hall of Japan, Inc., Tokyo

 Acknowledgments

I wish to thank my dear aunt, Louise Lyons Wolf, who edited and helped in every way in the creation of this book, and my dear children, Karen and Amy, just for being themselves.

A special thanks goes to those who helped prepare this book, each in her own way—Charlotte Leighton, Donna Roazen and Lorraine Doherty.

CONTENTS

 Introduction

I am a fat girl. The "now" picture you see on the cover is of a manufactured product. I carved myself out of a lump of fat, and so can you.

I had never acknowledged, not even to myself, that I was unhappy about being heavy. I was used to it; I was born fat. There is, however, a point in everyone's weight beyond which she is not willing to go. The lucky (thin) person panics at 115; some of us don't become frantic until the scale strains above 200.

My friends and family could not understand why I was fat. They never saw me eat. Of course not! I wouldn't dream of munching when people were around. During a social evening I wouldn't touch a smidgen of candy or a sliver of cake, but as soon as the company left, I went to work on every goodie in sight!

In the days when I weighed between 140 and 150, I felt that I could still be called pleasingly plump. But let's face it—when you're five feet tall, you're more plump than pleasing. It was when I went above this "norm" that I used to try every fad diet on record.

I went on a banana diet. Have you tried that one? For days I ate nothing but bananas and skim milk. If I disliked this combination to begin with, I *loathed* it before the week was up. As an additional penalty, I gained three pounds. Later I learned that aside from being inadequate in nutrients, if enough of these two foods are eaten, they are quite apt to add more pounds than they subtract.

Of course I tried pills—hasn't everyone? They made me feel as though my heart was going to beat out of my body, taking the top of my head with it. They also pinned down my arms and legs so I couldn't move. As you yourself may have experienced, after the first two weeks, pills no longer work as effective appetite suppressants. They do give you pep, and that is the reason so many dieters are dependent on them. The pill addict is afraid of not being able to get out of bed in the morning or function without them. Pills can also cause extreme nervousness, tenseness and irritability, and should be taken only under the supervision of a physician.

One of my neighbors who borrowed a friend's prescription felt certain she had found a simple solution to her weight problem. At first she lost her appetite and about five pounds a week. Then she also lost her sense of humor, her temper and her friends. When her husband started threatening to disappear, she was sensible enough to throw away the pills and make a real effort to satisfy her appetite with non-fattening foods. After six months on the Special Diet, she was 47 pounds lighter and in the best of health emotionally and physically.

People who claim that the whole-meal-diet drinks are as delicious as chocolate milk shakes must have warped taste buds. I bought a whole case once in a determined effort, but after sampling a variety of powdered vitamins in a chocolate or coffee or strawberry base, I decided not to add drinking to my eating problems.

I loved the "Fat Diet." Having been a great fat eater all my life, I found it a natural for me. I could eat as much as I liked of tuna and sardines in oil. If the principle behind this diet was that you would eventually be nauseated by the intake of all that fat, it was a failure in my case—I wallowed in it. When I buttered my bread, the butter was as thick as the bread. (Old friends who remember my growing "up" days recall me as "Bread and Butter in the Kitchen Drawer, Lois"—that's where I used to hide it.) I had even convinced myself that this fat was necessary for me. Surely there must be something in my physical makeup that required a great deal of "quick energy"! How we do deceive ourselves! Never have I been as energetic as I am at present, and I take in no extraneous fat at all. I find oil distasteful to me now. The oil in tuna gives me heartburn, and the oil in salad dressing makes me feel greasy. I wish this indigestion to each of you.

I got fatter on the "Fat Diet." I gave up and decided again that I was meant to be fat. However, about six years ago my weight reached a new high, in diametric contrast to my spirits.

Insofar as a fat person is concerned, the old adage, "Opportunity Knocks but Once" is utter nonsense. Every day we have opportunities to do something for ourselves that could change our lives for the better. Although it may be true that you should have started dieting yesterday, it is not too late to start today. I would like to point out further that a failure today does not allow you to throw away the opportunity or to consider the day "gone." Failing success today, remember Scarlett O'Hara—there is always tomorrow.

My "tomorrow" happened on an evening when I went to my usual bridge game. When I opened the door everyone was waiting for me. I was asked to sit down. They wanted to speak to me. I knew that I had had it. I had trumped my partner's trick once too often. But when the words came, they were something like this: "Lois, you must do something about yourself . . .

you look as if you've been taken to the gas station and pumped full of air. Each week you grow larger and larger. We're afraid you're going to burst."

This experience would have been even more humiliating were it not for the fact that, unknown to my friends, I had already taken the first important step toward "doing something" with myself. I had made an appointment with an internist and promised myself that I would follow his advice even if it meant living on bread and water for the next month.

After my examination, I sat down in the doctor's office prepared for the worst. He gave me the usual lecture about how my eating habits were damaging my health, and then suggested that I join a weight-reducing group. I said, "That's ridiculous! The group diet allows you 1200 calories a day! I *gain* weight on 1200 calories! Besides, I don't eat fruit, fish, eggs or vegetables, and I don't drink milk, and these are foods you *must* have on the group diet." Since my blood pressure was quite high, the doctor agreed to let me go on his "Stinker Diet" of 800 calories. I leave to your imagination the state of my nerves—a chronic overeater stuck with four shrimp for dinner! It was civilized torture. I had to hold my chair when the food went by. But I was determined; and I was rewarded by a loss of 4 pounds the first two weeks and 2 pounds the second two weeks (without cheating). After that a state of diminishing returns set in until the day when there was no loss at all. (Incidentally, each time I lost weight my blood pressure receded until it became normal.)

I was satisfied. I had reached my favorite weight. This may not have been satisfactory by anyone else's standards, but to me it was simply great. I was happy. I decided to go to a group to learn how to maintain the weight level.

When I attended the group meeting for the first time I was not impressed. The topic of the day was "Appearance" and how important it is in everyday and professional life. The lecturer said: "No man turns around to look at a dumpy female; he turns to look at a trim, well-groomed woman. People think more of you if you look like a person who takes care of herself."

To me, this was absurd. I had led a normal life. My fat hadn't held me back in any of my ventures: social, marriage, motherhood or career. But how could I be sure? Only now can I accept the fact that it is natural for people to place their confidence in individuals who look as if they have self-control and willpower. Without ever articulating it, there are those who in their social as well as business endeavors react negatively to fat men and women. Many doors are closed to obese candidates for an important position, regardless of their talents and qualifications. In this age of "appearance worship," it is becoming increasingly difficult for an overweight person to accomplish the breakthrough that would bring his abilities to the foreground much faster if he looked the part.

Apart from the impression your appearance makes on other people is the glorious feeling of self-confidence you experience when you know you look well. This alone can help a person to succeed.

Melvin F., an insurance salesman who lost 67 pounds on the Special Diet, attributes his impressive new home to his trimmer physique. While he once hid his girth behind a desk, he now gets out where he can meet people, earn their confidence and be of help in planning their future security. Whereas before he flinched when he quoted longevity statistics, he now can speak with authority. Without those 67 pounds of fat to tote around, Mel has lowered his golf score, gained a reputation for being the kind of man who gets things done and, even more important, discovered that living is more fun when you have the desire and energy to work at it.

But, getting back to the group diet, I followed it as conscientiously as I had followed the banana, the "Fat," the pill regimen and the Stinker Diet. To my surprise and delight I was not hungry the whole week! When I weighed in and the scales indicated that I had lost 3½ pounds, I was absolutely flabbergasted (blubbergasted?). In my whole life I had never lost so much in one week. When no one was looking I kept sneaking back on the scale to re-weigh and be reassured. I was so thrilled that I actually tingled with joy. It was a miracle.

Re-education of Eating Habits Can Take Place Only by Learning Substitution

I am a compulsive eater. Perhaps you are, too. I eat when I am hungry; I eat when I am not hungry. I eat when I am unhappy, and I eat when I am content. I eat when I feel unappreciated and also when I feel loved. I don't need an excuse for eating—I eat all the time!

For my kind of eater there has to be a Special Diet. I venture to say that anyone with a normal thyroid who eats under any or all of the above circumstances and does not follow a Special Diet designed to handle his problem will get fatter and fatter.

Maybe there was an excuse for some of us to be fat when we had to starve to lose. But with our Special Diet, starvation is a deterrent to weight loss. One of the secrets of the success of the plan is that you can, if you wish, eat throughout the day. There is always something to eat—at any hour—so that we compulsive eaters can always satisfy our craving for food with snacks that help to produce energy instead of fat. Once you give up foods that are the nibbler's nemesis, such as potato chips, and substitute raw vegetables, your loss of weight will be balanced by the self-respect you gain—and don't turn up your nose at raw vegetables until you've tried crisp chunks of celery seasoned with garlic salt.

People who are thin were not born under special stars. There are as few people who stay slender because of glandular conditions as there are people who are fat because of malfunctioning glands. Individuals who are thin work at it.

Some individuals *seem* to be able to eat everything. My husband is one of these. He is a thin man and he eats correctly. He eats slowly and has good table manners. Unlike many fat people, he never talks with his mouth full, nor does he reach for "seconds." If there should be a snippet of fat on his meat, he conducts surgery right on his plate to remove it. I am sure you are familiar with the nursery rhyme about Jack Spratt and his wife. We were the personification of that rhyme. It goes without saying that he always leaves something on his plate. In the past that "something" would never reach the garbage pail—I ate it. I used to perform this same inelegant task for my children, under the misguided notion that food eaten standing at the sink "doesn't count."

When I was convinced that I had finally discovered a diet that satisfied my hunger pangs and also permitted me to use a little ingenuity in the kitchen, it was almost impossible for me to talk about anything else. After years of preparing recipes for sauces and strudels, I was soon making some of my favorite dishes with the ingredients that appeared on the diet list. Within a matter of months, for the first time in my life, standing in front of a mirror in a fitting room was no longer a traumatic experience; it was a joy.

Inasmuch as I belong to the Clean Plate Club, the Special Diet suits my disposition exactly. It is required that I eat everything on my plate. This permits me to almost forget that I'm dieting and just concentrate on enjoying good foods.

Part of the success of the program—the major part— can be credited to the sane and sensible principles behind it and the satisfaction derived from the allowed foods. The Special Diet is a social diet. When we go to a restaurant we can eat regular portions. We do not have to be martyrs or draw attention to ourselves as dieters. Because this is not a low-carbohydrate diet, our bodies do not crave candies, pie or cake; and when a pastry tray is passed we have the physical resistance to refuse a piece.

Baked goods have tipped the scales in the wrong direction for many of my friends. For a week or two they would munch contentedly on their lettuce leaves and lamb chops. Then the need for something sweet would far surpass their desires for slimmer figures. Of course, after they devoured the first cupcake, the damage was done, and whatever diet they happened to be following would come to an untimely end.

By requiring that you eat bread at breakfast and at lunch, and by insisting that you drink milk, the Special Diet provides your body with the carbohydrates it requires and alleviates the craving for sweets.

We have many things going for us. We can make selections from every course. To dine out and to order jellied madrilene, steamed clams, salad, lobster and half a cantaloupe, as I did recently, is not exactly deprivation. If lobster had not been my choice, then steak, roast beef, lamb chops or fish could have been substituted. No one was aware that I am a dieter because it was not obvious from the size of my portions, nor by the variety of the foods I ate.

On our Special Diet we eat a lot. We are never hungry, and certainly not being hungry is a tremendous bonus. The recipes, as outlined in the following chapters, can make our so-called diet foods taste very good. Until I went on the Special Diet, I never ate fish, fruit, eggs or milk. But once I learned how to prepare these foods in new and different ways, I also learned to like them. People on any number of programs can enjoy our food with impunity—gall bladder patients, low-calorie dieters, spastic stomach sufferers, diabetics and people who have to be on a low-cholesterol diet.

I must mention here how much better I feel since being on the Special Diet. Let me tell you that most fat people are not brimming over with good health. Many overweight men and women are even ill-nourished. Although they eat a great deal, their diet is far from well-balanced, nutritionally speaking.

Because fat people overload their digestive systems, they often have one or more digestive complaints. It's either acid indigestion or heartburn, or a pain in the back or a pain in the chest. The Special Diet is not a cure-all, but you will find certain symptoms greatly alleviated if you are conscientious about staying on the program. My digestive system no longer answers me back. We are on excellent terms—it enjoys the food company I keep.

Before going on the Special Diet I experienced a low point every afternoon. I *had* to take a nap. Some fat people I know have difficulty getting out of bed in the morning, and if they do manage to crawl out, they pop right back as soon as the children are off to school.

When you eat properly, when you are on a high protein diet, you not only look better but you feel better, which is even more important. A high protein diet gives you the sustained energy you need and, in addition, it creates for you a wonderful sense of well-being.

You have read countless times that you must change your eating habits. Benjamin Franklin is reported to have said, "To lengthen life, lessen thy meals." This lesson in arithmetic is one we should all learn. It wouldn't hurt to write it out and tape it onto a full-length mirror. This should help with double motivation—the motivation of seeing ourselves perhaps heavier than we would like to be, and the motivation prompted by the promise of a longer life.

The question is, has anyone told you exactly how to change the eating pattern of a lifetime? The Special Diet will help you to achieve this relatively simple but vital element in weight reduction and maintenance. By merely extending the same basic diet, you can branch out and still remain well-nourished and "safe." You will stay thin because of the way you have learned to cook and eat.

If someone else in your family needed the help of a special diet to feel well, I'm sure you would go to any length to help him achieve this goal. You must do this for yourself, for your own sake as well as for the sake of your family. If you don't take care of yourself, who will do it for you?

When I lost weight I felt I had accomplished something of which I could be proud, something only I could do for myself. This feeling of pride, self-respect and achievement can also be yours.

ONE
CAUSES THAT
CONTRIBUTE TO OBESITY

❧Environment

Certain cultural backgrounds put emphasis on rich foods. In Jewish and Italian homes, for example, a degree of insult is felt when food is left over or refused. Such an atmosphere leaves its mark on a child, for it is not only acceptable to eat but it is highly desirable and a social advantage. This is only one way in which the environment plays a part in the creation of eating habits. Try this one on your memory—I'm sure it will have a familiar ring. From the background comes the sound of a child crying . . . high-heeled footsteps running toward the sound . . . soothing voice saying, "Don't cry, honey, Mommy will give you a cookie." Food here is proffered as a direct comfort, so is it any wonder that throughout our lives we look upon food as a source of solace?

Martha D., a member of my bridge club, once confessed that whenever she found a dress she especially liked, she usually bought it in two sizes because her weight constantly bounced up and down. Upon questioning her, I learned that when she was a child her father always gave her candy as a reward for various accomplishments. As an adult, she established a pattern of buying herself a box of chocolates whenever she felt that a treat was deserved. Giving a dinner party, cleaning the house, doing a heavy load of laundry, finding someone to mow the lawn—these and other small triumphs were all accomplishments that, in Martha's opinion, should be and were rewarded. And as she added accomplishments to her list, she also added pounds to her figure. Fortunately, before she gained too much, vanity came to the rescue. It was extremely difficult for Martha to give up the treats and adhere to a diet, but she persevered and lost 10 pounds. This was a *real* accomplishment that called for a celebration—a reward—a *big* box of candy, which in turn was followed by a return to old eating habits. This was also the start of a vicious circle. Martha diets until she can fit comfortably into her size 10 clothes, then enjoys the treats of her childhood until it's necessary for her to wear the size 12's. Then back she goes on her diet. Although Martha's story is indicative of how environment can cause a weight problem, her solution is definitely not recommended.

One other environmental factor comes to mind. Many people I have met say to me: "Would you believe that when I was a youngster I had to go to a special camp to be fattened up? And now look at me!" When I look, I usually see a person with 50 pounds or more to lose. Yes, I believe it. I have met women 65 years old who are still eating to please their long-departed mothers who, in days of childhood, used to plead with them to "take just a little more mashed potatoes."

At this point I make a plea on behalf of your children and grandchildren. It is impossible for one human being to judge the extent of hunger or the degree of appetite experienced by another. Don't force your child to eat. When he is hungry he will voluntarily take in all the food he wants or needs. No one willingly starves himself. Don't make their consumption or rejection of the food you offer a prime factor in your approval or disapproval of the young people in your family.

➤Economics

A certain economic climate is reflected in "Eat all you can—who knows when, or if, more will be coming?" Generally, the foods most readily available are the starches, which not only contribute to obesity but contribute to malnutrition as well. Even if and when the economic situation improves, the eat-all-you-can habit continues. There are adults who stuff themselves as though food were going out of style by midnight. This type of gluttony is usually the result of an economically deprived childhood.

Shirley G. grew up during the depression years. Her family had enough food to eat, but there was none to waste. Shirley's parents frequently reminded their children of how fortunate they were and pointed out the people who had to stand in line for a bowl of soup or had to sell apples on street corners. The scarcity of food and fear of having to go hungry left an indelible impression on Shirley. Even after marrying a successful lawyer, she was unable to bring herself to leave the slightest morsel of food uneaten. Inasmuch as her husband liked to see a variety of foods on the table, there was always an abundance of leftovers for Shirley to dispose of. Within four years of marriage she was more than 40 pounds overweight. She tried crash dieting, but having accustomed her body to expect large quantities of food, it couldn't be satisfied by grapefruit and hard-boiled eggs. The Special Diet was conceived for the Shirleys of this world. It satisfies their needs and, by adding a few frills to the basic menus, it also provides the entire family with meals that are appetizing and nourishing.

⇝Monotony

Most of us have known at least one lithe and lovely young woman who "let herself go" after she got married or after the birth of her children. Perhaps her added responsibility, the sameness of the housework routine or too much time spent at home and in the kitchen have caused her to resort to fattening snacks to help relieve the frustration of her "tied-down" feeling. Throughout the day she seeks comfort or consolation in that extra cup of coffee that has to have "something to go with it." A new interest or hobby will usually help these faulty eating habits.

For people who enjoy good food, cooking is probably the most interesting of all hobbies. Preparing meals from the foods listed on the Special Diet is a pleasurable challenge that's a sure cure for boredom.

⇝Occupation

I have genuine sympathy for overweight people who own ice cream parlors or delicatessens or bake shops or who work in any of these places. They are surrounded by temptations wherever they turn. Their situation is not hopeless, however. I have known people who were able to lose successfully even when they had to spend their whole day in gourmet shops where they handled delicacies of every description.

Suzanne G. managed a tearoom that specialized in the most beautiful desserts in the city. After the lunch-hour rush, she always sat down to relax and sample an over-sized piece of pie or cake. After she went on the Special Diet, Suzanne solved the problem of her coffee break by convincing the bakery chef to try some of the recipes for diet desserts. As Suzanne's figure improved, so did the tearoom's luncheon business, and their diet desserts are now as famous as their towering layer cakes.

If you belong in this category where fattening foods are an occupational hazard, remember that your handicap has been licked by others, so don't start eating the wrong foods out of despair or unnecessary defeatism.

≥Immobility

Bedridden people have, perforce, a marked decrease in activity which, coupled with boredom, may cause them to overeat. This combination of decrease in the expenditure of energy and desire to eat need not cause added weight. By following the Special Diet, one can actually lose. When my mother broke her ankle she was immobilized for over a month. In spite of this, by adhering to the Special Diet she was able to lose weight at the rate of 1 ½ to 2 pounds a week.

≥Boredom

When Evelyn D. came to New York from the Midwest, she found a job with a small investment firm. Most business was transacted by telephone, and so although her days were busy and interesting, there was little opportunity to meet people and make friends at business. Being shy by nature and not having many friends in the city, Evelyn formed the habit of going straight home from work, fixing herself a cocktail and then eating a solitary dinner in front of her TV set. Boredom and the proximity of the refrigerator soon helped pad her already rather large frame with several layers of fat.

Vanity plus a shortness of breath convinced Evelyn that she should take off weight, so she started to skip breakfast. When she didn't get the desired results she started skimping on lunches. The next step was to limit herself to a small steak or two hard-boiled eggs for dinner and clear all of the snack foods out of the refrigerator. Unfortunately she didn't clear out the liquor cabinet. Scotch on the rocks replaced the before-dinner cocktail, and more, many more, drinks were substituted for the refrigerated snack foods.

When I was introduced to Evelyn she had just been released from the hospital where she had been treated for malnutrition. Excess weight was still a problem, but Evelyn's doctor had convinced her that she should reduce by eating well-balanced meals. In other words, the Special Diet was just what the doctor ordered, and it has proven to be effective.

It's not uncommon for many people to eat because they have nothing else to do. Lacking the initiative or self-confidence that is needed to seek out activities that will stimulate their interest, they may center their lives around a refrigerator—or what is even more dangerous, a liquor cabinet.

Anxieties, social upsets, domestic difficulties or even being alone send some of us straight to the refrigerator or to the cookie jar. Knowledge of what we can eat with safety (no weight increase) will keep us from becoming victims of our craving for food while under tension.

❧Glandular Imbalance

In rare instances where glandular disturbances exist, they are usually correctible when the prescribed dosage of thyroid is taken. If you are overweight the odds are 100 to 1 that you have no one to blame but yourself. On the other hand, if you have truly been true to your diet—haven't cheated even once —see your physician. Don't, under any circumstances, attempt to diagnose your condition. Thyroid pills or extracts must be taken under strict medical supervision and only when there are definite indications that this treatment is necessary.

⇒Subconscious Factors

For the orally oriented individual, food may be the balm that makes life tolerable. Victims of some causes that contribute to obesity claim they are afraid that if they were to change their eating habits drastically their emotional problems would become more devastating. My feeling is that, in some situations, being slim may obtain those very things for you that are causing the frustrations, the anxiety and the tendency to overcompensate.

While we were in college, Peg S. was one of those so-called "jolly fat girls" who was always invited to parties for laughs. She made the usual jokes about "Omar, the tentmaker, designing her clothes, and needing a swimming pool for a bathtub, and not being able to find a husband who could afford to feed her." However, as one after another of her friends married, Peg's references to herself as "just a barrel of fun" were uttered in a voice far from merry.

After not having seen Peg for a number of years, we happened to meet in a restaurant. Following the usual gasps of recognition and exclamations of "how wonderful it is to see you," Peg stepped back to take another look at me. After measuring every inch of my silhouette with her eyes, she asked very sympathetically: "Lois, have you been ill? You're so thin." This called for an enthusiastic description of the Special Diet and a report on how wonderful I felt. Peg was dubious, but she listened. Within a week she called and asked if we could meet for lunch, because she wanted to know more about how I had lost weight. It took three or four meetings for me to convince her that yes, she could lose 50 pounds, and no, she would not have to starve herself.

We made arrangements to meet every week so that I could check on her progress and encourage her to continue. It was a slow process, but in time every last one of those 50 pounds disappeared. The transformation was amazing—for the first time I realized that Peg was a most attractive young woman. She also had a new vitality and the self-confidence that invites other people's interest. Probably one of my happiest and proudest moments was being matron of honor at Peg's wedding the following year.

Not only was the Special Diet perfect for Peg's weight problem, but I feel certain no other eating program could have been successful. Peg was, and still is, a big eater. The important thing about this particular program is that we never suggest you curb your overeating—we just want you to learn the substitution of the right foods for the damaging ones.

⋑Obesity and Your Children

There is an 80 per cent chance that a child will be fat if both parents are fat, and a 50 per cent chance if one parent is obese. Heredity? Not necessarily. More often, too many calories in the family meals are responsible for several members of a family being overweight. While heredity may play a part in obesity, weight can be controlled by what is kept in the refrigerator and put on the dinner table.

Your child is not pleased to have an overweight parent or parents. He wants a mother and father who look like everybody else's mother and father. He can brag about having a cuddly mommy for just so long before this loses its appeal.

Just because our children don't mention our being overweight doesn't mean that they aren't thinking and coming up with their own conclusions about obesity. One mother who approached her child as to why she wasn't informed of the monthly kindergarten parents' meetings was told, "But Mommy, I didn't think you'd fit in those little chairs!" In a similar vein, in another kindergarten class a teacher was passing out paper and crayons, requesting that each child draw a picture of his mother. One little boy said, "May I please have two pieces of paper? My mother is too big for one."

So our children are aware of how we look, and if possible we do want to spare them a lifetime of fighting the same weight problem we have waged. As cited, if you and your spouse are overweight, it is very possible that your child will also be heavy. If your child already shows signs of obesity, let's discuss a few more facts.

We have a mistaken belief that to be big is to be strong and healthy. We have a tendency to feed our children an excessive amount of food. This may cause an individual to be less, not more, physically and mentally alert. Obesity is just as deleterious to the health of children as it is to adults. Research indicates that the habit of overeating is acquired, not inherited.

It is exceedingly difficult to get children to adhere to a reducing diet. A child's world revolves around parties, holiday sweets and the weekly allowance his friends use for candy and ice cream. The best way you can help an overweight child is to have only the right foods around for him to nibble on and for his regular meals. The skinny members of your family can get their fattening foods away from home. Make the food as palatable as possible. Set a good example. Try to control your desire to nag. Remember, *you* had to learn by your own experience, and it took you quite a while.

TWO

THE DIET

⋙ The Plan for Women

➤BREAKFAST

4 ounces orange, grapefruit or tomato juice (or any fruit)

1 egg or 2 ounces cottage cheese (scale weight) or 2 ounces fish or 1 ounce hard cheese *

1 slice (1 ounce) enriched white or whole-grain bread

Beverage

➤LUNCH

3 ounces cooked fish or poultry or 2 eggs or 6 ounces cottage cheese (scale weight) or 2 ounces hard cheese

* Hard cheese is defined as clearly sliceable cheese.

All you want of the Unlimited Vegetables
1 slice (1 ounce) enriched white or whole-grain bread
Beverage
Fruit (have any time)

➔DINNER

6 ounces cooked meat, fish or poultry
All you want of the Unlimited Vegetables
4 ounces of the Limited Vegetables
Beverage
Fruit (have any time)

➔IN BETWEEN

2 cups skim milk or buttermilk or 1 cup evaporated
skim milk (*Note:* 6 ounces plain part-skim yogurt
may be substituted for 1 cup milk)

➔*The Plan for Men*

➔BREAKFAST

4 ounces orange, grapefruit or tomato juice (or any
fruit)
1 egg or 3 ounces cottage cheese (scale weight) **or**
2 ounces fish or 1 ounce hard cheese (sliceable)
2 slices (2 ounces) enriched white or whole-grain bread
Beverage

➔LUNCH

4 ounces cooked fish or poultry or 2 eggs or 6 ounces
cottage cheese (scale weight) or 2 ounces hard
cheese (sliceable)

All you want of the Unlimited Vegetables
2 slices (2 ounces) enriched white or whole-grain bread
Beverage
Fruit (have any time)

8 ounces cooked meat, fish or poultry
All you want of the Unlimited Vegetables
4 ounces of the Limited Vegetables
Beverage
Fruit (have any time)

➔IN BETWEEN

2 cups skim milk or buttermilk or 1 cup evaporated
    skim milk (*Note:* 6 ounces plain part-skim yogurt
    may be substituted for 1 cup milk)
2 additional fruits

➦*The Plan for Teenage Girls*

➔BREAKFAST

4 ounces orange, grapefruit or tomato juice (or any
    fruit)
1 egg or 2 ounces cottage cheese (scale weight) or
    2 ounces fish or 1 ounce hard cheese (sliceable)
1 slice (1 ounce) enriched white or whole-grain bread
Beverage

➔LUNCH

3 ounces cooked fish or poultry, or 2 eggs, or 6 ounces
    cottage cheese (scale weight) or 2 ounces hard
    cheese (sliceable)

All you want of the Unlimited Vegetables
2 slices (2 ounces) enriched white or whole-grain bread
Beverage
Fruit (have any time)

➔DINNER

6 ounces cooked meat, fish or poultry
All you want of the Unlimited Vegetables
4 ounces of the Limited Vegetables
Beverage
Fruit (have any time)

➔IN BETWEEN

4 cups skim milk or buttermilk or 2 cups evaporated
    skim milk (*Note:* 6 ounces plain part-skim yogurt
    may be substituted for 1 cup milk)
1 additional fruit

➔*The Plan for Teenage Boys*

➔BREAKFAST

4 ounces orange, grapefruit or tomato juice (or any
    fruit)
1 egg or 3 ounces cottage cheese (scale weight) or
    2 ounces fish or 1 ounce hard cheese (sliceable)
2 slices (2 ounces) enriched white or whole-grain bread
Beverage

➔LUNCH

4 ounces cooked fish or poultry or 2 eggs or 6 ounces
    cottage cheese (scale weight) or 2 ounces hard
    cheese (sliceable)

All you want of the Unlimited Vegetables
2 slices (2 ounces) enriched white or whole-grain bread
Beverage
Fruit (have any time)

➔DINNER

6 ounces cooked meat, fish or poultry
All you want of the Unlimited Vegetables
4 ounces of the Limited Vegetables
Beverage
Fruit (have any time)

➔IN BETWEEN

4 cups skim milk or buttermilk or 2 cups evaporated
   skim milk (*Note:* 6 ounces plain part-skim yogurt
   may be substituted for 1 cup of milk)
1 additional fruit

➔UNLIMITED VEGETABLES
A must *for lunch and dinner—you may also have them
at any other time during the day.*

Asparagus	Endive
Bean Sprouts	Escarole
Broccoli	Kale
Cabbage	Lettuce
Cauliflower	Mushrooms
Celery	Onions, Raw
Chard	Parsley
Chinese Cabbage	Peppers
Cucumber	Pickles

Pimentos

Radishes

Rhubarb

Sauerkraut

Spinach

String Beans,
    Frenched

Summer Squash

Turnip Greens

Watercress

Zucchini

→LIMITED VEGETABLES

Artichokes

Bamboo Shoots

Beets

Brussels Sprouts

Carrots

Eggplant

Kohlrabi

Leeks

Okra

Onions, Cooked

Peas

Pumpkin

Rutabagas

Scallions

Squash, Winter

String Beans

Tomatoes

Tomato Sauce (2 ounces)

Turnips

Water Chestnuts

→TOP PRIORITY MEATS,
POULTRY, FISH
(*Lowest in calories*)

Bass

Brains

Chicken breast

Clams

Cod

Crab

Flounder

Finnan haddie

Haddock

Halibut

Heart
Lobster
Kidney
Mussels
Oysters
Pike

Scallops
Shrimp
Sturgeon
Sweetbreads
Trout (brook)
Weakfish

➔SECOND CHOICE

Bluefish
Bonito
Butterfish
Chicken (dark meat)
Liver
Mackerel
Salmon (canned)
Sardines (without oil)

Shad
Shad roe
Swordfish
Trout (lake)
Tuna
Turkey (light meat)
Veal
Whitefish

➔THIRD CHOICE
(Three times a week only [cumulative])

Any kind of beef, fresh salmon, dark meat turkey, lamb, all-beef frankfurters, tongue

➔FREE FOODS
(Use at any time in any quantity)

Low-calorie carbonated beverages, bouillon, salt, pepper, paprika, herbs, spices, horseradish, lemon, lime, tea, coffee, 12 ounces tomato juice, vinegar, water, mustard, soy sauce, clear soup, 2 thin slices of tomato for lunch

➤DON'TS FOR DIETERS

Alcoholic beverages
Avocados
Bacon
Butter
Cake
Candy
Chinese food
  (regular style)
Chocolate
Coconut
Cookies
Corn
Crackers
Donuts
Dressings (except
  dietetic)
Dried fruits
Fried foods
Gravy
Honey
Ice cream, ices
Jam
Jelly
Lentils
Lima beans

Macaroni
Margarine
Marmalade
Mayonnaise
Noodles
Nuts
Oil
Olives
Pancakes
Peanut butter
Pies
Popcorn
Potato chips
Potatoes
Pretzels
Puddings
Rice
Soda water (regular)
Soy beans
Spaghetti
Sugar
Sweet or sour cream
Syrups
Waffles

➔FRUIT

Our definition of a fruit would be any medium-size apple, pear, orange, nectarine, plum, etc., or any of the following: 4 ounces unsweetened juice, ½ cantaloupe, 12 strawberries, ½ cup blueberries, 1 cup cranberries, 2-inch wedge honeydew, ½ grapefruit, ¼ pineapple, 1 small banana.

➔How to Follow the Diet

A recent government survey made at Fort Dix, N.J., indicated that over a six-month period, drugs used to inhibit appetites were of no help to dieters. I do not believe in taking any form of appetite depressant—most of us tried them and, if you remember, there were no lasting benefits. I know now that re-education of eating habits is the only sensible way to reduce. It takes time and patience to get results. We didn't get fat over-night, and neither will we be able to wake up within a few mornings looking like sylphs. By this I mean it is necessary to stay on a reduction program for at least six weeks, in accordance with the findings of the late Norman S. Jolliffe, M.D., Head of the New York Board of Health Obesity Clinic.

If, for medical reasons, you *require* thyroid and/or a diuretic, then you must take the prescribed medication and follow your doctor's advice. It is always best to check with him before start-ing any weight-loss endeavor. Once you have your doctor's approval, invite the neighborhood children in and empty your candy dish and cookie jar into their eager little hands. You will then be ready to take off weight by following an eating program that is more pleasant than you can possibly imagine.

You will never be hungry on the Special Diet. There is always something to eat at any time of the day or night, so if you feel the need for food—eat. Since it is the act of snacking itself, and not what the snack consists of, that matters to the compulsive eater, you'll be perfectly satisfied and happy. I personally snack a great deal on the unlimited vegetables—crisp, cold and well-seasoned. Some of my friends save the fruit they would ordinarily have at breakfast for later in the morning. Others have their luncheon dessert with their afternoon cup of tea. One of the enjoyable plus factors of the Special Diet is that you don't have to train your appetite to adhere to a time schedule.

Don't skip any meals. It is a fallacy to think that you are saving calories. With the right food you won't experience the let-down feeling that usually results in a consuming craving for the wrong kind of food.

Weigh your protein and limited vegetables. The purchase of a postal scale will be your only necessary expense, and when you have become thin you can use it for weighing letters. (And you'll be sending plenty of letters in answer to your fan mail!)

Women must have three fruits a day; five is the number for men (it's a man's world) and four for teenagers. All dieters must exclude cherries, watermelon, dried fruits and grapes. But don't let this make you feel deprived—there are still many delicious fruits to choose from that will add variety to each day's diet.

During each day (you may choose the time), you must have two glasses (four for children and teenagers) of skim milk or buttermilk. According to recent material published by the American Dietetic Association, milk should be included in a reducing diet because of its "high content of protein, calcium and riboflavin."

If you want to drink skim milk plain or flavored with coffee, sweetener, extracts, etc., remember that it should be made up and chilled several hours prior to use. It tastes best this way. If you dislike drinking milk, as I do, measure out ⅔ cup of dry skim milk (the woman's allotment) or 1⅓ cups (children's and teenagers' allotment) and use this dry milk in the various recipes you'll find throughout the book. Fluid non-fat milk is permitted on the Special Diet. Remember that whatever skim milk goes into your coffee must be deducted from your day's total. Many people hate buttermilk on sight. Try sweetening it and adding lemon extract. This is a milk of a different flavor. It is also good in preparing dressings.

You may use the Top Priority and Second Choice meats, poultry and fish interchangeably. Bear in mind that the Top Priority selections are lower in calories than the Second Choice and that it is suggested you have fish five times a week, either for breakfast, lunch or dinner. At least twice during the week it is recommended that fish be served for dinner.

Fortunately, during the past few years fish has become a favorite dish of many Americans. The availability of a large variety of ocean-fresh seafood in the supermarket freezer cabinets, a better knowledge of the innumerable ways in which fish can be prepared, and a greater awareness of the health-giving benefits of this fabulous food have contributed to its popularity. Nutritionists and physicians urge us to eat seafood more often because of its unique nutritional advantages.

Insofar as protein is concerned, few foods can compare with seafood. In addition to supplying energy, protein builds body tissue and helps fight infection. Seafood contains *complete* protein. This means the protein in seafood supplies the essential amino acids, those your body cannot manufacture and must get from the foods you eat.

Fish are rich in Vitamins A, D and K. An average serving of seafood provides 10 per cent of the daily adult Vitamin A requirement and all of the Vitamin D. The important B-complex vitamins are also present in seafood. A serving of seafood gives you about 10 per cent of this thiamine, 15 per cent of the riboflavin and 50 per cent of niacin you require each day.

A rich abundance of minerals is also found in fish. Iodine, magnesium, calcium, phosphorus, iron, potassium and copper are all present and help build strong bones and muscles and pretty teeth. Minerals are essential for building red blood cells and regulating body functions. For the dieter, fish isn't merely treasure from the sea, it's a gift from heaven—endowed with protein, vitamins and minerals and low, low in calories.

Equally important, seafood is one of the most versatile of foods. Recipes for preparing it are practically endless, so it adds welcome variety to diets. The one thing you should remember about seafood cookery is that fish and shellfish should not be overcooked as this spoils the flavor and texture. When a fish flakes at the touch of a fork, it is done. (Be sure to test it at the thickest part—where it takes longest to cook.) When the meat of a fish or shellfish is opaque instead of translucent, it is ready to eat. While following any timetable for cooking fish, it is wise to start checking for doneness *halfway* through the suggested cooking time. The mark of a good cook and a successful dieter is the ability to cook seafood properly and with a little imagination.

When you come down to the Third Choice selections, remember that these foods can be eaten only three times a week. In other words, choose from this list just three times a week.

Underneath the Third Choices are the "Free Foods." Know them—they are your friends. A low-calorie carbonated beverage is not just something to drink—it is also something with which you can bake apples and can make a gelatine dessert. The only way you can find out about this is by reading *all* of the recipes.

On the Special Diet you may not substitute. If it's not on the schedule, assume you may not have it during the time you are reducing. Five crackers may be equivalent to one slice of bread calorically, but crackers have more shortening, and the bread has the added desirable feature of being enriched. On a calorie diet you may substitute a piece of candy for a slice of bread. Not so on ours. The type of satisfaction you get from candy is not long-lasting. Bread provides vitamins and satiety—its energy lasts. As for butter and other fats, forget them for the duration.

Don't start comparing the calories contained in forbidden foods. If you keep thinking about the goodies you can't have, it only makes it more difficult to follow the diet and enjoy the many delicious foods it permits you to enjoy. It also makes it easier to rationalize cheating, and once that starts you're headed for trouble. Just forget about calories until you've lost your weight. Otherwise you will only be reinforcing your old bad eating habits. The diet will be easy for you if you let it become a non-varying routine experience—not that the foods you eat each day must be the same (in fact, they *should not* be the same), but the foods you *avoid* must be consistent so that you will establish new and beneficial habits. Cheating is a habit too. If you stay on the diet 100 per cent without cheating for two or three weeks, it will get easier and easier to get thinner and thinner. The Special Diet will then become part of your normal routine since it is neither a skimpy carbohydrate plan nor any other crash-type program.

If you find that you are getting bored after a month or so of being on the Special Diet, don't blame the diet—blame your cooking. With an infinite variety of spices to use—all of them "Free Foods"—there is no reason to feel restricted. If you own a cookbook that contains an herb and spice chart, study it. A pinch of nutmeg, a sprinkling of thyme or a hint of the many other seasoning agents you'll discover on the spice shelves of your food store will introduce a world of flavor into your diet. Many of my friends who have followed the Special Diet are better cooks now than they ever were before! If you are bored—start reading and cooking.

Some dieters enjoy being martyrs. I think the martyr type is doomed to failure. I consider it risky to have the wrong kind of food in the house. By the wrong kind of food I don't mean cookies per se—I mean only those cookies that will get to you. They will eventually be your downfall. When I make brownies, even if I quickly freeze them, there appears in my head a little light that keeps switching on and off, saying, "Lois, there are frozen brownies in the freezer." And I *like* frozen brownies. This is the kind of food I can't have around.

At this point I often get the argument that you *have* to have the figure-destroying treats around because your family asks for them. Nonsense. If your family is fat they don't need them, and if they're thin they probably don't want them. If they must have goodies, they can get them somewhere else. I used to have cake in the house and no one would touch it—a day would go by, two days, three days, and then . . . I *like* stale cake!

What do you do with a box of chocolates that arrives as a gift? Before you're tempted to break the seal, get it out of the house—give it to a neighbor, the postman or even a stranger who happens to be walking by. But don't even take off the outer wrapping if chocolate happens to be your hang-up. As for the cake you may feel duty bound to serve your guests—send whatever is left over home with one of them.

Don't test your willpower. (If it were so great, you would never have had a weight problem.) It makes the reducing program less attractive and puts unnecessary pressure on you. Remember, you're the important one; your whole family needs you.

Another dieting tip is to weigh yourself only once a week. Because of water balance and imbalance there is daily fluctuation. When you see the scale go down after you've cheated, you feel you can get away with something, and you go on to cheat again, often with disastrous and demoralizing results. Or if the water balance is working in the other direction, you'll see a gain after being as good as an angel, and then you'll get hysterical. (At least I did.) In the passage of a week's time, this balance is usually stabilized and it's much less confusing and discouraging for you to weigh at specified intervals, rather than trying to figure out day by day if a gain or a loss is due to water or your performance. Dieting is never easy—why make it harder for yourself with daily weighing? On your weekly encounter with the scale, be sure that you weigh in at the same time of day, in the same state of dress or undress. In the meantime, weigh your food, not yourself.

When you finish this chapter, plan to go shopping. We won't deceive you by claiming that the Special Diet is inexpensive. It isn't. But it also costs money to be fat—a *lot* of money. Add it up: the bakery bill, the liquor bill, the pill bill, the special wardrobe bill, the doctor bill, etc., etc. It's much wiser to spend it on prudent food selections that can help make reducing more enjoyable and which will make it unnecessary to incur the other bills. The challenge of finding and trying new foods is one of the things that can make your diet a stimulating experience. Buy all of the unlimited vegetables and canned fish you like. Stock up on the many delicious low-calorie carbonated beverages. Get some herbed vinegars and all of those exotic spices you've been meaning to use. Prowl around the fancy food stores and treat yourself to some of those good flavorings and extracts that you seldom see in the supermarket. (They'll come in handy for the milkshake and ice cream recipes.) The right food must be on hand. *It must also be ready for you to eat!*

Have your snacks and rewards *made in advance.* Make them the night before or early in the morning. Keep a plastic bag filled with crisp, bite-size pieces of celery, mushrooms, radishes, cucumber and other raw vegetables ready to pop into your mouth the second you crave something to munch on. While your breakfast coffee is brewing, whip up a frothy instant mousse for your mid-morning or late afternoon snack. Have an appetizing bowl of dietetic gelatine in your refrigerator at all times. We borrow the Boy Scout's motto: "Be Prepared." It's too late to start fixing some goodie for yourself *after* the need arises! Your food must be in the same state of availability as the forbidden cookie—ready to chew on at the first sign of hunger.

Men cannot live on compliments alone, and neither can women. Or can they? Actually it does make it easier to pass up the Cherries Flambé if someone has just told you that you're a better-looking dish. This is one of the rewards of your accomplishment, and also one of the morale builders that will help you keep the weight off.

This does not mean that you will never again have any goodies. What a desolating pronouncement that would be! What we hope is that you will become a discriminating eater—one who will not automatically reach out for some fattening food just because it's there, but rather one who will eat it because you really want it.

Many times I have gone over to an hors d'oeuvres table ready to dig in, but after taking one bite of a limp frankfurter encased in a blob of half-baked dough, I found it easy to turn my back on such untempting tidbits. They weren't worth the waste of calories. I have also found that two pieces of chocolate—chosen carefully, eaten slowly with rapture—can be much more satisfying than my previous habit of gobbling up half a box without actually tasting it.

Once you have reached your ideal weight you should never allow yourself to gain more than two pounds. If your weekly weigh-in day is Wednesday, try to weigh the same every Wednesday, although you may be at the peak (two pounds heavier) on Sunday. If by Wednesday you are not down to the right weight, be very strict about keeping on the Special Diet until you get your weight down again.

It is not advisable to do down five pounds under goal in order to have "play." I have seen too many people try this and the results were unfortunate. There is too much freedom—the discipline becomes too relaxed and so do you.

I have a friend who occasionally passed up refreshments with the comment, "Not tonight, I'm trying to take off two pounds." In the fat past whenever she said this I used to cringe. She made me feel as if someone had found me digging into a strawberry shortcake with a shovel. I took this as a personal affront, a device to embarrass me into becoming more conscious of my overweight. After all, what were her two pounds compared to my forty plus? I know now that she was exceedingly wise. You must get rid of the two pounds before they become three, then five and ultimately forty or more. Now I, too, lower the boom on two extra pounds, and then they never become two and a half, much less five or more.

When people reach their goal they are apt to feel they can relax—that their weight problem has been solved. I'm sorry to tell you this is not the case. The battle against weight can never be over. However, once you've won that first skirmish you have a strong ally on your side—pride.

I could never understand the old maxim, "Pride goeth before

a fall." In my opinion, justifiable pride is one of the most valuable assets a person can have. When you have dieted, exerted self-discipline and exercised willpower, you should feel proud of your accomplishment. Pride of accomplishment is a most enviable state of being.

The companion piece—pride in your appearance and in your new-found figure—should become your fighting weapon against backsliding. According to my philosophy, that old maxim should be reversed to read, "When pride goes, the fall cometh."

A maintenance diet must be well-balanced and carefully planned. To a certain extent it can be based on individual tastes and preferences, but be extremely cautious when you decide you're ready to become your own dietician, disciplinarian and reward committee. Some of my friends find that they can maintain their weight level by staying on the Special Diet from Monday to Friday, and then eating whatever they please during the weekend. Others have worked out different timetables for their feast or famine periods. I am not one of these. I enjoy the the security of being on the Special Diet every day and merely adding a cookie, a pretzel, a small piece of cake—whatever I happen to want—one goodie per day. Make a study of various maintenance routines, try them and then determine which is best for you. Just be sure that it *works* by checking it out by weighing yourself on the same day of the week, *every week*.

Don't think for one minute that the lid of the cakebox is now open to you. Remember Pandora! You must still maintain control and discipline. Remember you are on your own. Your friends and relatives will give you permission to go off your diet. They will even egg you on. "It's OK now—there's no need to be a fanatic." "No one diets in my house." "No one diets on a Saturday night." "Look, I made this pie just for you." "Please, just try a bit of Harry's birthday cake.'" "Look who's dieting!" are but a few of the persuasions and cajoleries that will be used to lure you from your path. Remember that it's your body and your health and nobody has the right to give you permission to stop taking care of yourself. Only *you* will know if it's okay to say yes. Trust your own judgment exclusively. Human nature is often paradoxical—the very people who urged you in the past to lose weight are now the ones who want to see some crack in the armor of your willpower. And they will be the first to make a snide remark if you look as though you have gained a few pounds.

⇒ Maintenance

You can learn to maintain your weight, but only under the following conditions.

1. You have reached your weight goal by being on a sensible diet.
2. You have re-educated your eating habits.
3. You enjoy being slim and want to stay that way.

People often say to me, "How can you stand the thought of being on a diet for the rest of your life? It isn't fair!" It's true, I agree—it isn't fair. But life isn't fair. It isn't fair for a diabetic to be on a diet for the rest of her life, or for a person who is troubled by an ulcer to eat in a special way. There are many people who have to follow a particular pattern of eating—those who are troubled by high blood pressure, gall bladder, gout, and so on. But all of these people know that there is an immediate punishment for going off their diet, a punishment that usually comes in the form of pain. And this is a strong deterrent to cheating.

If there was an immediate painful punishment for going off a reducing diet, it might help to keep us on the straight to be narrow. Instead we must concentrate on the positive. I am so grateful to be thin that I don't complain about my Special Diet —I automatically reach for the right food. The reward of admiring glances is far more satisfying than any food could possibly be.

⥤Exercise

I have found that exercise plays little part in weight reduction for sedentary obese people. It does, however, have three functions of some import. The first is that it increases circulation, which is important to people who are overweight. Secondly, it improves muscle tone. So-called spot reducing is actually a firming of a particular set of muscles. Although these may result in an apparent figure change, the change lasts only as long as you continue to do the exercises. The third and most important factor is that exercise gives you the feeling that you are doing something for yourself.

Once your muscles are toned up for the day, they stay toned up. Therefore it isn't necessary to repeat the series more than once each day. Each exercise is done three times. All are executed while seated in a straight chair with feet flat on the floor. A suggested time would be mid-morning.

1. Relax body downward. Raise yourself very slowly, putting arms to the side of your head. Lower shoulders and move head back three times.
2. Place hands on chin. Make fish-like movements by jutting your jaw forward three times.
3. Put arms to one side. Reach back three times and then come back to starting position. Put arms to other side and repeat.
4. Place hands on your abdomen so as to feel yourself breathe through the diaphragm. Breathe in—push stomach out. Exhale, pull stomach in.

5. Grip the sides of your chair. At the count of three, pretend there is a tack on the seat and jump up, tucking buttocks under.

6. Lift your left leg. Point toe. Raise leg as high as you can. Repeat with right leg.

7. Lift left leg. Rotate your ankle to the right three times. Rotate to the left three times. Repeat with right leg.

8. Stamp your feet.

9. Curl fingers backward from wrist. Bend trunk down toward floor and lift up, pulling arms upward and back until elbows are level with your shoulders. Pull arms toward back three times.

10. Extend arms straight to the side, level with your shoulders. Push two imaginary walls as hard as possible. Hold for six seconds. Relax. Repeat three times.

THREE

BREAKFAST

➤ *Introduction*

If you have a child who has attended the second grade,
you know how much importance is placed on eating the
"right" breakfast. An attractive and nutritionally balanced morning meal is believed by doctors and nutritionists to be essential
for energy. It "stokes the engine" and "gets us going," so to
speak. Studies have definitely indicated that those children who
eat a good breakfast are better achievers than those who skimp
or skip. I have found, also, that pre-school children are far less
irritable and difficult in the morning if persuaded to eat a substantial breakfast. This state of affairs is mutually beneficial to
child and mother—especially mother. What is true for children
holds true for adults as well.

It may interest you to know that many fat people skip breakfast because they think they are "saving" calories that way.
(I'm sure this doesn't surprise you at all. As a matter of fact,

don't you try it yourself now and then?) Not only is this caloric "saving" fallacious at the outset, but the felony is compounded by our doubling up on calories for lunch or by snacking at 11 A.M. or thereabouts on the nearest edible, which invariably just happens to be a sweet roll, a donut or some other destructive goodie to dunk with our coffee. It's amazing what this kind of unnecessary famished state will do. Fat or thin, all my life I have loathed cream or sugar in my coffee. I like it black or not at all. But when I let those 11 A.M. "hungries" go to work, I'd find myself with sugar and cream in my coffee because I felt I "needed" the extra energy, and I would drink it down even though I hated the taste! Along with my pastry, of course.

Grace F. had convinced herself that it was impossible for her swallow a mouthful of food before she left for the office. But when the morning coffee wagon came around, she was its best customer. An hour later she would shuffle out to the candy-dispensing machine, and then there was time for another "coffee plus" break before she started talking someone into joining her for a spaghetti lunch at the Italian restaurant. Day after day Grace managed to spend more than double the number of calories it would have cost her to have a well-balanced break-fast in the morning.

Making her realize that she could not lose weight if she con-tinued to skip breakfast wasn't easy. Her first argument was that she couldn't "bear to see an egg staring up at her in the morning." By showing her the Special Diet breakfast menus, I won that argument in a hurry. Then she complained that she'd have to get up an hour earlier to prepare and eat a full breakfast. It was difficult to make her accept the fact that the right food would make her feel more bright-eyed and ready to face the world than a little extra sleep—besides she would only have to set the alarm a half an hour earlier. If she hadn't been desperately anxious to lose weight, I might have found it impossible to get Grace to try the Special Diet. She did a good bit of balking, but eventually she followed the program to the letter. Within three weeks she lost 10 pounds, and then over the next four months she lost an additional 22 pounds. At the same time, her efficiency in the office improved, and that, plus her more attractive appearance, led to a more responsible position with a nice salary increase.

Grace's story is not unique. If you look around any large office you'll notice that many of the people who snack throughout the day on sweets appear to be tired. Although sweets have a certain energy value, it is short-lasting and they add little to a diet except calories. Now take another look at the staff in a busy office and you'll see that the majority of the people holding down executive positions have a trim appearance and the vitality that goes along with it.

A correct diet, reducing or maintenance, requires a good breakfast. When I was fat, like Grace I couldn't bear to look at food in the morning. I thought this indicated a certain estheticism in me. The trouble is, fat people never *look* esthetic, and what a hard time we have convincing the critical world that we are. Now I look forward to my first meal of the day. What fun, at last, to look as esthetic, trim and shapely, as I have always wanted to look, while at the same time I can enjoy eating a substantial breakfast!

If you like a conventional breakfast, we have it for you. If conventional breakfasts bore you, cheer up; we have provided quite a few different ideas for the first meal of the day. I have included conventional, not-so-conventional and some quick one-course repasts. You may choose whatever type breakfast you like depending on your mood. When I am hungry I separate everything, making each allowed item a definite and important course by itself. When I am not too hungry, I concentrate everything together. Therefore breakfast menus are listed under two categories: The first category contains suggestions for those mornings when you wake up feeling ravenous, and the second category is for days when your appetite would prefer to nap until noon. I cannot stress too often the importance of variety and experimentation, so try *everything* at least once.

(*Note:* All breakfasts are based on the women's and teenage girls' plan and will serve one person unless otherwise noted and include *all* the Special Diet requirements of protein, carbohydrate and fruit. Men and teenage boys are entitled to a second slice of bread, and if cottage cheese is their choice, an additional ounce.)

―――――――――――――――――

So You Like a Hearty Breakfast!

I know people who are so used to eating a large breakfast that this single habit was their undoing when they tried other diets. If you like to eat well at the first meal of the day, how about trying this for size (a smaller size for you, eventually).

Whole Quartered Orange
Cup of Bouillon
Salmon Salad
Coffee

Salmon Salad

½ head lettuce
2 ounces canned salmon, drained
2 tablespoons cider vinegar
2 tablespoons hot beef bouillon
1 slice bread, toasted and cut into croutons

Shred lettuce. Toss with salmon, vinegar, bouillon and croutons. Variation: Try tuna.

This is dieting?

So you're used to Danish pastry or sweet rolls in the morning! Admittedly this menu is a substitute, but I recommend it to those of you who have an early morning sweet tooth.

Danish Pastry
with
Blueberry Jam
Coffee

Danish Pastry

Beat two egg whites until stiff (this is your entire protein allowance for breakfast). Gradually add bread that you have toasted and whirled in the blender to make crumbs. Add 4 packs of sweetener. Drop by the tablespoon onto a cookie sheet. Bake in a 325° oven until hot and serve with ½ cup homemade blueberry jam and coffee.

Blueberry Jam   (TWO FRUIT SERVINGS)

½ packet unflavored gelatine
½ cup cold water
1½ cups hot water
3 tablespoons lemon juice
1½ teaspoons liquid sweetener
1 cup blueberries

➤Soften gelatine in cold water—dissolve with hot water. Add lemon juice and sweetener. Chill until syrupy. Add berries. Mix and chill.

Variation:

Substitute raspberries.

Many people find an egg a satisfying breakfast. You can scramble them and there is no need for Teflon—a heavy skillet or a double boiler will do. You can "fry" them the same way.

Baked Grapefruit
1 Egg, fried and sprinkled with seasoned salt
Coffee
Toast

Baked Grapefruit

Cut grapefruit in half and slice into sections. Remove membranes so as to allow as much cavity space as possible. Bake at 325° for 15 minutes.

Tomato juice adds zest to the flavor of your breakfast egg and adds variety to your diet.

Tomato-Egg Drop Soup
Whole Wheat Toast
½ Cantaloupe
Tea

Tomato-Egg Drop Soup

1 cup chicken broth
4 ounces tomato juice
1 well-beaten egg

Boil chicken broth with tomato juice. When boiling rapidly, drop in beaten egg.

This is the best I have. You'll never believe the quantity or the quality of this recipe until you try it. Pancakes were never so great—you'll feel guilty eating them. Makes three large pancakes.

Apple Pancakes
Coffee

Apple Pancakes

> 1 egg
> ½ cup liquid skim milk
> 1 slice bread
> 2 packs sweetener
> ½ teaspoon cinnamon
> 1 apple sliced razor thin

Blend everything together except apple. Add apple to batter. Pour ⅓ of batter into a Teflon pan or a heavy skillet. Flip, cook and serve. (After trying both pans, I found that from the standpoint of flavor a heavy skillet gives better results than the Teflon pan. There was no sticking, either.)

Variations:

1. *Add ½ teaspoon grated orange peel.*
2. *Fill with Diet Workshop Strawberry Jam and roll up like a crepe.*
3. *Substitute buttermilk for skim milk.*

Here's a breakfast to delight the dieting gourmet. What's more, it's quick and simple to prepare.

Tomato Juice
Welsh Rarebit on Toast Points
Melon Balls
Hot Coffee Frappé

Welsh Rarebit

Tear one ounce of American cheese into pieces and put in saucepan with ⅓ cup liquid skim milk. Add a few drops of Worcestershire sauce and sprinkle in a few grains of dry mustard. Place over low flame and stir thoroughly until melted. Toast white bread. Cut into triangles. Pour rarebit on top.

Hot Coffee Frappé

Blend together:

⅓ *cup skim milk powder*
½ *teaspoon instant coffee powder*
½ *teaspoon vanilla extract*
2 *teaspoons liquid artificial sweetener*
¾ *cup hot water*

If you're really hungry, take your favorite unlimited vegetable —even if it's bean sprouts—mix it up with 2 ounces of cottage cheese, salt and pepper. Add bread you have toasted and cut in cubes, and mix all together.

Cottage Cheese with Vegetables
Cinnamon Pear
Café au Lait

Cinnamon Pear

Cook together the juice of canned dietetic pears with ½ teaspoon red food color, and add a cinnamon stick. Boil together for five minutes. Pour over pears. Let pears set overnight. Voilà!

Café au Lait

Mix together 1 teaspoon powdered instant coffee and ½ cup hot water. Stir this into ½ cup skim milk. Heat together.

Who would believe anyone could eat like this and still lose weight? Well, you will after you've been on the Special Diet for a few weeks and see how pleasant it can be to rid yourself of excess pounds.

Strawberries with Sour Cream
Toast
Coffee

Sour Cream, Diet Workshop

2 ounces cottage cheese
2½ tablespoons buttermilk

Blend cheese and buttermilk together to make "sour cream." Mix strawberries in. Add artificial sweetener if you like. (You will find that many supermarkets stock a great product—frozen whole strawberries packed in a polyethylene bag, with no sugar added.)

Dieting is hardly a hardship when you wake up to a meal like this.

Dietetic Pineapple Slices
"Lox" and Eggs
Toast with Strawberry Jam
Coffee

"*Lox*" *and Eggs*   (SIX PROTEIN SERVINGS)

Well, not really lox, but close enough. This could be a show-off company breakfast.

¼ *cup green pepper*
2 *chicken bouillon cubes*
½ *teaspoon onion powder*
2 *tablespoons water*
6 *ounces red salmon (skin, bone and oil removed)*
3 *eggs*

Sauté green pepper with bouillon cubes and onion powder in water. When tender add salmon and cook until heated through. Scramble in eggs.

Strawberry Jam

½ packet unflavored gelatine
½ cup cold water
1¼ cups hot water
3 tablespoons lemon juice
1½ teaspoons liquid sweetener
1 cup crushed fresh strawberries

Soften gelatine in cold water; dissolve in hot water. Add juice and sweetener. Chill until syrupy. Add strawberries. Blend and chill.

The Italians enjoy a great breakfast—they call it Pepper and Eggs. It is a Sunday morning favorite.

Pepper and Eggs
½ Cup Dietetic Apricots
Strong Black Coffee

Pepper and Eggs

1 large pepper
¼ cup double-strength bouillon
1 egg
1 tablespoon cold water
Salt and pepper to taste

Parboil pepper. Cut in pieces and sauté in bouillon. When soft, add egg that has been beaten with cold water, salt and pepper. Scramble.

I Can't Stand to Look at Food in the Morning!

People who say they have no time to eat have no excuse once they have read this recipe. You can drink your breakfast at any time—while shaving or preparing breakfast for the rest of the family.

Instant Breakfast—Our Style

Blend together:
⅓ cup skim milk powder
½ teaspoon vanilla
½ cup dietetic peaches
¾ cup water
1 egg
1 slice enriched white bread

————————————————

How simple can it get? Take a slice of American cheese. Place on a piece of toast. Broil.

Grapefruit Juice
Grilled Cheese
Tea

Grilled Cheese

1 ounce yellow American cheese
1 slice toast

Place cheese on toast and broil until brown and crusty. Or—using thinly sliced bread, make a sandwich. Wrap in aluminum foil and *iron* until bread is toasted and cheese is melted. Or—using Teflon pan, pan broil sandwich until desired result is obtained.

Cream cheese and jelly are not gone forever...

Cream Cheese and Jelly on Toast
Baked Apple
Coffee

Cream Cheese   (SIX PROTEIN SERVINGS)

> 1 packet unflavored gelatine
> ¼ cup cold water
> ½ cup liquid skim milk
> ¼ cup buttermilk
> ½ teaspoon liquid sweetener
> 2 drops butter flavoring
> 12 ounces cottage cheese
> 2 drops Worcestershire sauce

Soften gelatine in cold water. Heat very slowly. Add everything else. Blend and beat. Chill. Top with Diet Workshop Strawberry Jam.

Baked Apple

> Core 12 apples. Place in baking dish and sprinkle cinnamon in hole of each apple. Pour 16 ounces of low-calorie black cherry soda over. Bake until tender at 325°.

Many-sided in its versatility, cottage cheese makes a perfect breakfast—perfect in content because of its protein and carbo-hydrates, and perfectly delicious when prepared according to this recipe.

Cranberry Juice   (LOW-CALORIE)
Cottage Cheese Special
Coffee

Cottage Cheese Special

>   2 *ounces cottage cheese*
> ½ *teaspoon grated orange peel*
> ¼ *teaspoon vanilla*
> ¼ *teaspoon cinnamon*

:➥Mix together. Bake on toast.

➥————————————————◀

Change lethargy to energy by starting the day with this light, protein-rich breakfast.

Unsweetened Pineapple Juice
French Toast
Coffee

French Toast

>   1 *egg*
>   1 *pack artificial sweetener*
> ½ *teaspoon vanilla*

:➥Beat egg, adding sweetener and vanilla. This gives it the special taste you admire in those restaurants that specialize in this kind of goodie. Soak bread and "fry" in Teflon pan or heavy skillet.

This breakfast is much too good to rush. Before you make yourself comfortable, boil extra water so that you can enjoy a second cup of tea.

2-inch Wedge Honeydew
Seasoned Farmer Cheese
Spiced Tea

Seasoned Farmer Cheese

Choose whole-grain bread for a change. Its chewy texture and nutlike kernels will be a pleasing and satisfying change to you. Toast bread and mound 2 ounces of farmer cheese on top. Sprinkle with seasoned salt and broil for 5 minutes.

Variation:

If you can find it, try Matke Ser (mother's cheese). It is firmer than farmer cheese and has more character.

Spiced Tea

This tea comes replete with orange peel, cinnamon and other lovely spices. Its marvelous aroma is a picker-upper in itself. And try it iced on a hot summer day.

Following my philosophy of putting things together to make them seem smaller and less to eat when you are not too hungry . . .

Orange Juice
Baked Egg
Coffee

Baked Egg

1 egg, separated
1 slice enriched white bread
Grated American cheese food
Pepper

Beat egg white until stiff. Spread on bread, making a slight hollow in center. Fill with unbroken yolk. Sprinkle with grated American cheese food and some freshly ground pepper. Bake 15 minutes in a 350° oven. (This can be converted easily into a lunch recipe by placing one ounce of American cheese under the egg white.)

The basis of this breakfast is cold jellied fish, and the recipe is presented here in quantity because it keeps a long time and the rest of your family may enjoy it too. It can be frozen, and I recommend this whenever possible. You can use it for breakfast, lunch or dinner—just weigh out the proper amount for each meal.

Grapefruit Sections
Pickled Fish
Toast
Tea

Pickled Fish

> 2 *cups cold water*
> 2 *teaspoons onion powder*
> 1 *teaspoon salt*
> 1½ *cups vinegar*
> 2 *pounds carp*
> *Artificial sweetener to taste*

Bring water to a boil with onion powder, salt and vinegar. Add fish and cook for ¾ of an hour. Take fish out and cool. Add sweetener to liquid and pour over fish. Chill.

If you're an anti-breakfast person, it's quite probable that it's the thought of cooking that makes you lose your appetite. Here's a way to get the day off to a happy start without going near the stove.

Apple Juice
Egg Nog
Toast

Egg Nog

> 1 egg
> ⅓ cup skim milk powder
> 4 packs artificial sweetener
> ⅓ cup water
> ½ teaspoon rum extract
> ½ teaspoon vanilla extract
> Dash of nutmeg
> 4 ice cubes

Blend all ingredients, except ice cubes, on lowest speed. Add cubes one at a time while machine is going. (In this way you will avoid getting the cubes stuck under the blades. According to the directions that come with most blenders, it is not to be used to crush ice cubes. However, it makes life so much simpler to use the blender for this purpose that when the blades get really dull I will have them sharpened, and consider the convenience worth it.)

Here's a real eye-opener for anyone who considers breakfast a dull meal. It's not when you eat nor how much you eat—it's what you eat that makes meals exciting and the Special Diet successful.

Grapefruit Juice
Smoky Spread
Coffee

Smoky Spread

1 ounce cottage cheese
1 ounce finnan haddie

➯Mash together. Spread on toast.

➯*Additional Breakfast Suggestions*

1. *Any cold leftover fish (especially swordfish) makes an excellent breakfast. I purposely plan to have it left over.*
2. *Hard, soft-boiled, or poached egg.*
3. *If you really hate breakfast, have a piece of fruit, a piece of toast and a custard.*
4. *If you are extremely hungry, start off with cream of mushroom soup.*

▓FOUR
LUNCH

⇒*Introduction*

Lunch is an easy meal to skip, but don't! Whether you are a housewife or an office worker, take the time to refuel your body's needs for energy. You wouldn't expect your car to run without gas, and neither will your body function at its peak performance without the addition of sustained energy in the form of protein. This holds true for everyone, but especially for the reducer. Going without lunch only means the onset of hunger pangs later in the day, resulting in an overladen dinner plate, or worse yet, an appropriating of a series of fattening snacks late in the day. Stop for a moment and reflect on all the heavy people you know (including yourself, perhaps?) who swear (truthfully) that they can go like a camel all day long without eating. They don't mention what they are eating from 10 P.M. until 2 A.M., and *that's* what's making them fat.

After her second baby was born, Laura B. gained 26 pounds within eight months. At age twenty-two her figure had taken on the matronly proportions of the middle-age woman who has "let herself go." During the winter, when fat had first started inching its way around her torso, Laura had excused it with the usual remarks: "I'm so bloated since the baby came." "We must find a new cleaner—this one shrinks everything." "Zippers aren't what they used to be—every time I pick up the baby they split wide open."

Then came the period when she hid her expanding girth under her husband's wool sport shirts saying they helped to keep her warm. Loose shifts and a full coat enabled her to get through the spring without having to make the admission that she was getting heavier by the day. Then came summer, a Fourth of July beach party, and last year's bathing suit that refused to budge beyond her knees. Laura couldn't kid herself any longer—she was FAT!

Why or how she had gained so much weight was difficult for her to comprehend. She didn't "care that much about food." The babies kept her so busy "there wasn't even time to eat." But after she studied her habits for a few days, she discovered that while she was getting a bottle out of the refrigerator, she also grabbed several slices of luncheon meat or some leftovers and ate them while standing at the stove. When holding the baby before he fell asleep, she usually sat next to a well-filled candy dish or a bowl of salted nuts and managed to empty it. Every time the two-year-old asked for a cookie, Laura put a few in the pocket of her apron so she could munch on them as she went about her household chores. No, she didn't ever sit down to a regular breakfast or lunch, but before her husband arrived home in the evening she managed to consume enough finger-foods to support the caloric needs of a farmhand.

Laura had to re-routine her days in an organized fashion before she was able to follow the Special Diet with any degree of success. Stopping for lunch was often inconvenient, but getting back into a size 7 dress made it well worth her while.

Remember that the most attractive curves result from three square meals a day. Lunch should be eaten approximately three to four hours after breakfast and four to five hours before dinner.

You will find that some days you are ravenous for lunch, and on other days you can take it or leave it. Now that you are committed to our program, you have no choice—you must take it, but you can choose a small edition if you like. Therefore, I have divided lunch into two categories for the at-home eaters—hungry lunches and not-too-hungry lunches. Lunch for people on the go will include restaurant eating and hints for lunch-bag carriers.

For the at-home eaters, I have found it helpful to make lunch a "party for one." It may sound silly, but I discovered over a long period of dieting that if I made my lunch as fancy as I could—using good plates, creating pleasing color combinations, preparing many courses, and waiting until after the children had been fed, and sitting down to it like a lady (by myself if necessary)—it made a difference. I came to look forward to my midday treat and felt like a V.I.P. Pamper yourself and let it be habit-forming.

(*Note:* All lunches are based on the women's plan and will serve one person unless otherwise noted, and include *all* the Special Diet requirements of protein, carbohydrate and fruit. For teenage girls, add a slice of bread. For teenage boys and men, add an additional slice of bread and one ounce of protein.)

At-Home Lunches— I'm Famished

Some of these recipes were improvised not only to feed the inner woman who demands quite a lot at lunchtime, but also because when expecting company I like to show off with the biggest lunch I can put together and still remain within the limits of the Special Diet. It never fails to delight me to hear, "Don't tell me you're on a diet when you eat all *this* for lunch." Of course I am, and this is what makes the Special Diet successful—the quality and quantity of the recipes. Try this one for raised eyebrows and questioning looks, and then go on, for there are more and more. By following the basics, once you have the knack, you can plan and execute your favorite foods to your own taste.

＊————————————＊

When there's a nip in the air this menu will satisfy your hunger for a more substantial lunch. It also appeases the dieter's secret craving for a big wedge of apple pie.

Clam and Bean Sprout Soup
Apple Pie
Coffee

Clam and Bean Sprout Soup

1 can bean sprouts
1 bouillon cube
3 ounces minced clams
    plus clam juice

Heat bean sprouts with bouillon cube and clam juice. Toss in clams. Stir and serve in colorful enameled bowls.

Apple Pie

1 slice bread
½ cup dietetic applesauce
Apple pie spice

Place bread under broiler and toast on one side only. Spread applesauce on untoasted side. Sprinkle with apple pie spice. Bake at 300° for 10 minutes.

This exotic Oriental-type lunch is guaranteed to help you hurry up the slimming-down process in a most pleasurable fashion.

Won Ton Soup Without
Egg Foo Yong
Toast
Mandarin Oranges   (DIETETIC)

Won Ton Soup Without

1½ cups water
 2 chicken bouillon cubes
 1 stalk celery, diagonally cut
 ¼ cup Chinese cabbage,
      diagonally cut
 ¼ cup mushrooms
 ½ cup torn fresh spinach

Heat water to boiling. Add bouillon cubes and stir until dissolved. Add celery and Chinese cabbage and cook five minutes. Add other ingredients, stir and serve.

Egg Foo Yong

½ cup bean sprouts, drained
½ cup canned mushrooms, drained
½ cup cooked green pepper
 1 teaspoon monosodium glutamate
½ teaspoon salt
    Dash ground pepper
    Dash garlic powder
 2 beaten eggs

Mix everything together and cook in heavy skillet until done.

The following is a rather unusual suggestion that I have included to meet the requirements of those who like their sweets; and let's face it, there are times when we'd hand over the family jewels for something sweet, creamy and satisfying. Here we have it, not in a half cup, not in a whole cup, but in the large two-cup variety size. Actually, we are using all of our protein and an entire day's milk supply for dessert, while the balance of lunch will consist of fruit, soup and bread.

Cantaloupe Fingers
Sauerkraut Soup
Custard
Whole Wheat Toast

Sauerkraut Soup

    ½ *cup sauerkraut*
    1 *cup tomato juice*

Mix and heat over low flame.

Custard

    2 *cups skim milk*
    2 *eggs*
    2 *packs artificial sweetener*
    1 *teaspoon vanilla*
    ¼ *teaspoon salt*
    ¼ *teaspoon nutmeg*

Scald milk in double boiler over boiling water. Beat eggs, then add sweetener, vanilla and salt. Add hot milk and mix well. Strain into cups. Sprinkle with nutmeg and set cups into water (water should reach only half way up the outside of the cups). Bake 1 hour at 300°.

Your bridge ladies are accustomed to something special and especially filling; something to eat with a knife and fork slowly so that there will be plenty of time for talking. Try this menu when it's your turn to be the luncheon hostess.

Cheesy Crabmeat
Strawberry Gelatine
Apple Cookies

Cheesy Crabmeat
(ONE PROTEIN SERVING; MULTIPLY AS REQUIRED)

1 slice white bread
4 asparagus stalks, cooked
1 slice American cheese (1 ounce)
¼ cup skim milk
1½ ounces crabmeat

Toast bread. Cover with cooked hot asparagus. Melt cheese in milk and add crabmeat. Cover asparagus with mixture.

Variations:

Use tuna or chicken in place of crabmeat.

Strawberry Gelatine

Use packaged dietetic strawberry gelatine, adding whole strawberries. Serve in champagne glasses.

Apple Cookies

  4 egg whites
  ⅔ cup skim milk powder
  1 teaspoon vanilla extract
  1 teaspoon strawberry extract
 4–6 packs artificial sweetener
  1 apple, grated
   Cinnamon

 Beat egg whites until stiff. Add skim milk powder and mix well. Add extracts, sweetener and apple. Spoondrop onto cookie sheet. Bake at 275° for 45 minutes. Remove from sheet and dust with cinnamon. Recipe contains the equivalent of 2 ounces of protein and entire day's milk supply. Reduce main course to compensate for amount eaten.

Your own Chef's Salad is going to be the start of a new fad for a summertime lunch. Put into it as much of the things you can eat in unlimited quantities as your appetite requires—lettuce, escarole, cucumbers, radishes, sliced peppers. Julienne 1 ounce of cheese and cube 1½ ounces of chicken. Place these on top. Make garlic croutons by slowly drying one slice of bread in the oven with garlic powder rubbed into the topside. Cut into one-inch squares. Toss salad with dressing and start munching.

Chef's Salad
Peach Ice Cream

Dressing

> 1 cup buttermilk
> 1 garlic clove, crushed
> Pinch chili powder (*optional*)
> ¼ teaspoon dry mustard
> ⅓ teaspoon cider vinegar
> Pinch curry powder (*optional*)

Blend all together.

Peach Ice Cream
(TWO FRUIT SERVINGS PLUS TWO MILK PORTIONS)

> ½ cup cold water
> 1 teaspoon liquid sweetener
> 2 mashed peaches
> ⅔ cup skim milk powder
> 1 teaspoon vanilla

Beat in mixer from 10 to 15 minutes. Place in freezer in a covered container.

Did you know that oysters are an excellent source of the "protective" nutrients—proteins, minerals and vitamins? Few foods are better balanced nutritionally, and yet oysters are exceptionally low in calories.

Oyster Stew
Toast Fingers
Fruit Compote

Oyster Stew

A clam is nice in its little cloister, but somehow I prefer the oyster—it's moister.

> Salt, pepper, garlic powder
> 1 cup skim milk
> 4 ounces oysters
> ½ cup canned mushrooms, drained

≥Add salt, pepper and garlic powder to liquid skim milk. Add oysters and mushrooms. Heat—don't boil.

Fruit Compote

Stew cut-up peeled apples and pears in any flavor low-calorie soda. Add a dash of cinnamon. Cool. Add fresh melon and cut-up pineapple. To determine one portion, divide the number of included fruits.

When you prepare this lunch, make sure you're really hungry.
It's far too good to leave even the tiniest bite uneaten.

Giant Omelette
Toast
Baked Pears

Giant Omelette

1 10-ounce package frozen spinach
1 4-ounce can mushrooms, stems
*   and pieces, drained*
2 eggs
*   Salt, pepper*
2 tablespoons cold water

❧Thaw a box of frozen spinach. Mix with a can of drained mushrooms. (I use the stems and pieces in almost all my recipes because the saving is great and my stomach doesn't know the difference.) Whip up two eggs with salt, pepper and cold water. Fry in a Teflon pan or cast iron skillet, adding spinach and mushrooms when the bottom layer is dry and brown. Cook for 5 minutes, then flip over or place under the broiler. Serve with toast.

Variations:

Use cooked zucchini in place of spinach.
Sprinkle with a bit of Parmesan cheese.

Baked Pears

Wash, core and halve pears. Place face up in
a baking dish. Cover with low-calorie black cherry
soda and bake at 325° for 1 hour.

Aloha—and here's a wiki wiki (that means fast) way to shape up for next season's luaus.

Polynesian Shrimp
Lemon Gelatine

Polynesian Shrimp   (TWO PROTEIN SERVINGS)

> 1 medium green pepper,
>   cut into 1" pieces
> 1 can beef broth
> 1 tablespoon soy sauce
> ½ cup pineapple juice
> 2 teaspoons lemon juice
> 6 ounces cooked shrimp
> ½ cup pineapple, sliced

Cook green pepper in small amount of broth for approximately 5 minutes. Remove from skillet and add all the rest of the ingredients. Stir and put on toast. If you're really hungry, arrange enticingly over a bed of hot bean sprouts on toast.

Lemon Gelatine

> 1 packet unflavored gelatine
> 1 cup cold water
> 7 packs artificial sweetener
> 1 cup hot water
> ¼ cup lemon juice

Soften gelatine in cold water. Add sweetener and hot water and stir until dissolved. Add lemon juice. Mix thoroughly. Pour into mold and chill.

We pride ourselves on running the international gamut, so let's continue with:

Company Blintzes
Perfection Salad
Apple Bettina

Company Blintzes   (TWO PROTEIN SERVINGS)

½ *cup liquid skim milk*
½ *cup skim milk powder*
2 *eggs*
½ *teaspoon salt*
⅛ *teaspoon pepper*
1 *pack artificial sweetener*

❧Stir the skim milk into skim milk powder and beat out all lumps. Beat eggs into mixture and add all remaining ingredients. Stir well. Pour batter into Teflon pan or heavy skillet to make a thin pancake, tipping the skillet to cover with batter. Brown and turn. (Both sides will brown in a matter of seconds.) Makes 6 eight-inch pancakes or 12 smaller ones.

Filling

6 *ounces cottage cheese*
½ *pack artificial sweetener*
Pinch salt
Pinch cinnamon
1 *egg white*

❧Blend all ingredients, mashing well. Divide filling and place on each pancake. Fold pancake into envelope shape. Heat through in oven at 325° and serve with Diet Workshop Strawberry or Blueberry Jam.

Perfection Salad

>   1 packet unflavored gelatine
>   ½ cup cold water
>   1 ½ cups hot water
>   2 chicken bouillon cubes
>   ¼ cup vinegar
>   ½ teaspoon salt
>   ¾ cup finely shredded cabbage
>   1 cup diced celery
>   1 pimento, chopped

Sprinkle gelatine on cold water to soften. Dissolve in hot water in which bouillon cubes have been dissolved with vinegar and salt. Chill until syrupy. Fold in vegetables. Turn into a one-quart mold or individual molds. Chill until firm.

Apple Bettina   (FOUR FRUIT SERVINGS)

>   4 apples
>   4 packs artificial sweetener
>   1 teaspoon cinnamon
>   4 slices toast, cubed

Mix together apples, sweetener and cinnamon and arrange in layers alternating with bread cubes, ending with bread. This can be baked in a plain pan covered with foil or in a Teflon pan. Serve with skim milk (dry) mixed with a small amount of water so that it has the consistency of cream.

The following recipe has been written up many times as my favorite lunch, as indeed it is. (One warning, however: Sometimes I find that people who are not losing well on the diet are eating too much hard cheese. Hard cheese is high in salt . . . try to limit it to 4 ounces a week.) I prefer it made with whole-grain bread.

Dieter's Pizza
Lime Gelatine Royale
Iced Tea

Dieter's Pizza

Toast a slice of bread, or 2 thin slices that together weigh one ounce. Top with as many roasted peppers as you desire, and then cover with two ounces of skim-milk Mozzarella cheese. (This sounds hard to get, but most mozzarella cheese is made of skim milk.) Sprinkle with garlic powder and oregano and bake until cheese melts. This tastes very good, is very impressive and, cut into smaller squares, can be used as an hors d'oeuvre for special company.

Variations:

Use mushrooms or mashed cooked zucchini squash. Provolone can be substituted for mozzarella cheese.

Lime Gelatine Royale   (THREE FRUIT SERVINGS)

½ honeydew
1 package dietetic lime gelatine
1 cup hot water
1 cup cold water

Using a melon scoop, form honeydew into balls. Mix lime gelatine with hot water. Add cold water. Cool until gelatine becomes syrupy. Add melon balls. Refrigerate until firm.

⮞Lunch ... Who Needs It?

If you are not too hungry at lunchtime, the following recipes are for you. You may, however, save your fruit or dessert until your afternoon low point. But don't skip lunch—it must be eaten because your body needs it! By eating what your body requires, you will not be vulnerable to eating the wrong thing when hunger strikes.

And no complaints about cooking for yourself being "too much trouble." You're right—it is a lot of trouble. It is a bore to shop and cook for oneself. Moreover, it is downright selfish at times. But what's wrong with that? You've earned a little consideration. After all that you've done for others, it's about time that you did something for yourself. You can't expect your family and friends to fully appreciate you until you develop some self-esteem. To quote Ralph Waldo Emerson, "Make the most of yourself, for that is all there is to you."

This tuna recipe may sound like an unorthodox mixture at first, but it grows on you so that you actually crave it. It is so delicious that it would not be out of place as a spread (on cucumber rounds) for a cocktail party. You must force yourself to try new things—we want you to get to like them to replace the foods we've removed from your old fattening diet.

It took me nearly a year to try this recipe. I knew I wouldn't like it. But I did try it, finally, and ever since I've been eating it several days a week.

Tuna and Cottage Cheese with Horseradish
Strawberry Sherbet

Tuna and Cottage Cheese with Horseradish
(TWO PROTEIN SERVINGS)

>   3 ounces tuna
>   6 ounces cottage cheese
>   1 teaspoon white horseradish
>   4 slices thin white bread, toasted

❧Carefully drain the oil from tuna. (If you wish, you may use the water-packed variety.) With fork, mix the tuna with cottage cheese and horseradish. Pack on toast.

Strawberry Sherbet   (FOUR FRUIT SERVINGS)

>   1 pint fresh strawberries, crushed
>   Juice from strawberries plus enough
>   water to make 2 cups
>   2 packs artificial sweetener
>   ¼ cup dry skim milk

❧Add sweetener to strawberry-water combination and stir until dissolved. Add dry milk. Blend and place in refrigerator tray. Place in freezer until it begins to freeze (about 45 minutes). Beat until fluffy in chilled bowl. Return to freezer in tray and *repeat* the procedure. Store in freezer.

Invite a friend to lunch and show off a little. She'll never suspect that this menu was designed for dieters unless you or your shapelier figure let her in on the secret.

Fish and Shrimp
Peach Cocktail

Fish and Shrimp   (TWO PROTEIN SERVINGS)

¼ cup chicken broth
4 ounces raw filet of sole
1 tablespoon onion flakes
7 cleaned shrimp (3 ounces)
1 cup sliced mushrooms
Salt, pepper
2 slices bread, toasted and
    crumbled
Chopped chives

Place broth in casserole dish. Put in the fish. Sprinkle with onion flakes and cover with shrimp and mushrooms. Sprinkle with salt and pepper. Add bread crumbs. Bake 20 minutes at 350°. Sprinkle with chives.

Peach Cocktail   (FOUR FRUIT SERVINGS)

2 cups diced fresh peaches
1½ teaspoons lemon juice
¼ cup low calorie ginger ale
Fresh mint
1 teaspoon liquid artificial sweetener

Combine peaches, lemon juice and sweetener. Spoon into champagne glass. Add one to two tablespoons ginger ale to each glass. Garnish with mint sprig.

For people who appreciate exquisite French cooking, nothing can quite take the place of Coquilles Saint-Jacques. Yet you'll have to admit that these stuffed clams are a delectable compromise.

Stuffed Clams
Pineapple Cup

Stuffed Clams

> 1½ ounces minced clams, drained
> 1 egg
> 1 teaspoon parsley
> One dash each of salt, oregano, garlic powder, grated Parmesan cheese

❧Combine everything except cheese and mix well. Put into aluminum clam shells and sprinkle with cheese. Bake at 375° for 25 minutes. (The shells can be purchased at most fish stores.) Serve with toast.

Pineapple Cup   (EIGHT FRUIT SERVINGS)

> 1 pineapple
> 2 cups diced orange
> Low-calorie orange soda
> Mint

❧Cut away outer skin of pineapple. Remove core and dice pineapple. Add diced orange. Mix with soda to taste. Serve in sherbet cups with a sprig of fresh mint.

The Special Diet enables you to vary your meals in the same way you vary your wardrobe—according to the season. This spectacular molded seafood salad followed by creamy smooth orange sherbet will help make summer's soaring temperatures feel several degrees cooler.

Seafood Salad
Orange Sherbet

Seafood Salad   (TWO PROTEIN SERVINGS)

> *1 package dietetic lemon gelatine*
> *¼ cup cold water*
> *1 teaspoon salt*
> *1½ cups boiling water*
> *2 teaspoons vinegar*
> *1 teaspoon onion powder*
> *6 ounces canned tuna, drained*
>   *and flaked*
> *2 tablespoons chopped celery*
> *2 tablespoons chopped green pepper*

Soften gelatine in cold water. Add salt and dissolve in boiling water. Stir in vinegar. Chill until thickened. Fold in remaining ingredients and pour into loaf pan. Chill until firm. Unmold on crisp greens. Place toast points around.

Orange Sherbet
(ONE MILK SERVING AND ONE FRUIT SERVING)

> *1 cup skim milk*
> *3 tablespoons orange concentrate*

Mix and freeze, stirring occasionally.

The following recipes are far too good to be secret. Invite a chubby friend to have lunch with you.

Zuppa Stracciatella
Creamed Mushrooms
Applesauce

Zuppa Stracciatella

>   *1 egg*
>   *1 ounce grated hard cheese*
>   *1 slice white toast, blended*
>   *to make crumbs*
>   *1½ cups beef bouillon*

Beat egg. Mix with cheese and crumbs. Stir into bouillon. Cook for 5 minutes.

Creamed Mushrooms

Cook fresh mushrooms in skim milk with salt, pepper, parsley and paprika.

Applesauce (SIX FRUIT SERVINGS)

>   *6 tart apples*
>   *¾ cup water*
>   *Artificial sweetener to taste*
>   *Dash cinnamon*
>   *½ teaspoon grated lemon peel*

Pare and core apples. Slice thin. Add just enough water to keep apples from sticking. Bring to a boil with sweetener and cinnamon. Cover. Simmer until apples are soft. Strain and add lemon peel.

The aroma of fresh pungent herbs, the flavor of a delicately seasoned omelette and the eye appeal of the grapefruit basket offers further proof that the Special Diet makes very good sense—to three of your five senses.

Omelette aux Fines Herbes
Grapefruit Baskets

Omelette aux Fines Herbes

¼ *teaspoon parsley*
¼ *teaspoon thyme*
¼ *teaspoon sweet basil*
¼ *teaspoon onion powder*
 2 *tablespoons water*
 2 *eggs*
¼ *teaspoon salt*
  Freshly ground pepper

Crush herbs and soak in water. Beat eggs slightly. Add herbs, water, salt, onion powder and pepper. Cook in heavy skillet. Fold. Garnish with parsley and serve with toast.

Grapefruit Baskets

Cut grapefruit in half, crosswise. Use a corer to remove center. Cut away segments. Sprinkle with artificial sweetener. Chill. Before serving, use a sharp pointed knife or scissors to cut a half-inch rim of shell all around, leaving segments untouched. Use rim for basket handle. Place a strawberry in the center of the fruit.

Regardless of what the sun is doing, the afternoon will seem brighter after this light and luscious lunch—especially when you remember that meals like this are helping to turn you into a rather light and luscious dish.

Tuna Mix
Strawberry Sponge

Tuna Mix

3 ounces tuna
1 tablespoon mustard
1 tablespoon tarragon vinegar
½ cup finely chopped lettuce

⮞Mix together all ingredients and serve on toast triangles.

Strawberry Sponge   (FOUR FRUIT SERVINGS)

1 packet unflavored gelatine
¼ cup cold water
1 tablespoon liquid artificial sweetener
1 tablespoon lemon juice
1 pint strawberries, crushed
2 egg whites

⮞In the top of a double boiler (or heavy pot) soften gelatine in water for 5 minutes. Add sweetener and lemon juice. Heat and stir until gelatine is dissolved. Remove from heat and add strawberries. Let stand until the mixture thickens. Beat until light and fluffy. Beat egg whites until stiff. Fold into gelatine mixture. Spoon into mold and chill. (Recipe contains the equivalent of 1 ounce of protein. Reduce main course to compensate for amount eaten.)

You may not get any sympathy from friends when they see you dieting on lunches like this, but you will get plenty of compliments when you appear in clothes that are two or three or more sizes smaller.

Seafood Croquettes
Cole Slaw
Orange Mold

Seafood Croquettes

> 1 slice white bread
> ¼ cup buttermilk
> 3 ounces any cooked fish
> ½ teaspoon chopped parsley
> Shake of sauté onion powder
> Salt and pepper

Soak bread in buttermilk until all the buttermilk has been absorbed. Mix in other ingredients and form into croquette shapes. Brown in skillet.

Cole Slaw

> 1 head cabbage, shredded
> 1 teaspoon dry mustard
> ¾ teaspoon salt
> ¾ cup buttermilk
> ⅓ cup cider vinegar
> ½ teaspoon pepper

Blend everything except cabbage. Toss with cabbage.
Optional additions: dill, curry, chili powder

Orange Mold (Four Fruit Servings)

> 2 packets unflavored gelatine
> 1 cup water
> 2 tablespoons orange rind
> 1 cup fresh orange juice
> 2 cups buttermilk
> 4 packs artificial sweetener
> 1 teaspoon vanilla
> 1 cup dietetic mandarin oranges

Soften gelatine in water and dissolve over low heat. Mix orange rind and juice, buttermilk, sweetener and vanilla. Add dissolved gelatine. Pour into one-quart mold until set. Unmold and decorate with oranges.

Horseradish is one of the wonderful "Free Foods" on the Special Diet, so let your taste buds decide the exact amount to use. If you like a really "heady" cocktail sauce, go ahead and live it up. The cool Orange and Lemon Ice will soothe your burning tongue.

Shrimp Cocktail
Orange and Lemon Ice

Shrimp Cocktail

> 6 ounces cooked shrimp
> Lettuce
> Toast fingers

Shrimp should be icy cold and placed in cocktail glasses surrounded by crisp lettuce and toast fingers. Arrange around small dish of cocktail sauce.

Cocktail Sauce

¼ cup tomato juice
1 teaspoon white horseradish
1 teaspoon lemon juice
½ teaspoon finely chopped parsley

Combine all ingredients and chill.

Orange and Lemon Ice

9 packs artificial sweetener
1 cup water
¼ cup lemon juice
1 egg white
Dash salt
1 orange, diced

Cook sweetener and water for 10 minutes. Cool. Add to lemon juice. Pour into ice tray and freeze until firm. Remove to chilled mixing bowl and beat with rotary beater until light and creamy. Beat egg white with salt. Fold in. Fold in orange. Return to tray and freeze.

Fish is a brain food! You may not get smarter from eating it, but you are much brainier when you do decide to make fish your dish.

Baked Fish
Melon Rings with Raspberries

Baked Fish

4 ounces raw flounder
1 cup tomato juice
1 green pepper, chopped
Sliced mushrooms
1 celery rib, diced
Salt, pepper
1 slice white bread

꩜Combine all ingredients except fish and cook for 15 minutes. Pour over fish. Bake 30 minutes at 350°.

Melon Rings with Raspberries   (FOUR FRUIT SERVINGS)

Cantaloupe
1 cup fresh red raspberries

꩜Peel melon and refrigerate in plastic bag. At serving time cut peeled melon into 4 one-inch rings. Place one ring on each serving plate. Fill center with ¼ cup raspberries.

ᴣLunch in a Restaurant

Having lunch in a restaurant is not so frustrating as you have been inclined to think. More and more restaurants are becoming aware that there are people with dietary restrictions. Even if the restaurant you happen to be in has made no effort to accommodate the requirements of the dieter, you will find *something* that is adaptable to your purpose.

One of my friends has made a list of restaurants within a five-block radius of her office and the foods they serve that are legal for dieters. I was surprised to see an Italian restaurant checked as one of her favorites. She explained that it features a special green salad chock-full of large tuna chunks. This, with a slice of bread, a wedge of melon and a cup of Italian coffee, not only conformed with the requirements of the Special Diet but was perfectly satisfying.

Sometimes I think the delicatessen is my favorite eating-out place. They usually have turkey roll (white meat) which is great. Three ounces of this, with mustard, lettuce and tomato, makes a walloping sandwich. Remember, too, that we are allowed a variety of cheeses on our diet, and the delicatessen is also equipped to provide these.

Any sandwich bar will have American cheese. You can ask the management to place it on toast and broil it, or you can eat it plain, with mustard and lettuce. Coffee shops usually have sliced chicken as well. Happily, most restaurants are stocked with small cans of tuna and salmon.

Small tea-room type restaurants will have cottage cheese and/or poached eggs available for your selection. The tea room is also the home of the cottage cheese-fruit salad plate that can be adapted nicely to your needs. And in most of the better restaurants, you can get broiled fish or roast chicken, and sliced white meat of turkey.

You may prefer a chicken and diced vegetable dish, cooked Chinese style, or shrimp and bean sprouts (without cornstarch or oil). This is easy to get in any Chinese restaurant—one of the preferred types of restaurants for the dieter. Another tip, eat with chopsticks—the food lasts longer that way!

If you should be stuck in a hamburger-cheeseburger-French-fry short-order kind of place (and try not to be), remember that you may order a broiled 3-ounce pattie of ground beef on a toasted roll and eat only half of the roll. It's better to have your third-choice meat at dinner when you can have more of it, but there may be times when you must settle for less.

⇛For Brown Baggers

Packing a lunch isn't too difficult. If you're a man or a teenager, you may take two slices of bread, as usual. If you're a woman, you can manage your one ounce of bread in any of three ways. A regular slice may be cut in half, or backed with a thick wedge of lettuce. Or you may have two slices of bread if they are thinly sliced. Weigh them on your postal scale; if they exceed one ounce, trim the crusts.

Mayonnaise is out, of course, but mustard or cottage cheese (seasoned or plain) will do very nicely as a spread. Some of the easiest sandwiches to make are:

*Sliced Chicken with
   Tomato
Sliced Cheese
Turkey Roll
Leftover Fish
Crabmeat, Cottage Cheese
   and Peppers*

*Chopped Chicken with India
   Relish
Chopped Egg and India Relish
Tuna and Chive Cottage Cheese
   Spread
Cold Veal Roast
Canned Chicken and Mustard
Canned Salmon and Pickles*

However, your lunch does not have to revolve around a sandwich. According to the wife of a businessman I know, if a hold-up man ever snatches her husband's handsome attaché case when he is walking to his office during the early morning hours, the criminal will reform on the spot. It seems that Paul L. personally packs an assortment of raw vegetables and fruits in individual plastic bags. He then carefully puts them along with a can of fish or chicken and a can of fruit juice into his attaché case and strides off briskly to business.

You may not be inclined to pack a lunch of such lavish proportions, but you can eat your bread as an accompaniment to easy-to-prepare foods such as:

> 3 ounces of cottage cheese mixed with 2 ounces
> of minced clams and ½ teaspoon each of
> Worcestershire sauce and onion powder
> 6 ounces of cottage cheese mixed with
> unlimited vegetables or ½ cup dietetic
> fruit cocktail
> 2 hard-boiled eggs (or deviled eggs)
> Cold chicken breast

Whatever combination you choose, be sure to include your protein, unlimited vegetables and a fruit (which you could eat during your coffee break). Many working people have brought wide-mouth short thermos jars to use for gelatine desserts. This really rounds out their lunch as it narrows down their hips.

FIVE

DINNER

⊋Introduction

I am a firm believer in a multi-course dinner. The more courses, the greater the variety in taste and texture, and the more eating enjoyment. In following the Special Diet, or any diet, success evolves from variety and quality. Away with the peeka-boo slice of beef of last year's diet—we're going to eat well and plentifully.

Dinner prepares you for the longest fast of the day, and no one needs much persuasion to eat this main meal. You may, however, need nudging to try new and different recipes. This is no mere steak, lettuce and tomatoes diet. That's too tedious, and too far away from your norm, whatever your norm may be. I know this much: If you enjoyed eating just steak, lettuce and tomatoes, you wouldn't be fat and reading this book in the first place. (What do people who eat only steak, tomatoes and lettuce want with a cookbook anyhow?)

So try something new, even if you *think* you won't like it. I frequently overhear people complaining that they "can't stand vegetables." They have my sympathy—not because they must eat vegetables on the Special Diet, but because they have lived so long without learning how to prepare some of nature's most valuable gifts. Vegetables are an important source of bulk in the diet and also provide many of the vitamins necessary for maintaining good health. Of course, if you're one of those people who drop a block of frozen vegetables into boiling water and then cook them until they are limp and tired-tasting, it would be amazing if you or anyone in your family could even bear the thought of a vegetable at dinner. But before you make any further statements regarding any of your "pet hate" foods, please, please try every recipe in this book and follow it exactly as given.

Incidentally, I have found that when I didn't like something the first time, if I tried it a couple of weeks or even months later, I may have changed my mind about it. Sometimes it's the mood you're in, or the mood your stove is in or a matter of not perfecting the recipe. The worst that can happen is that you actually won't like it, and then you can always dump it. The best that can happen is that you will have found something new to add to your roster of recipes—recipes that should be especially good to compensate for those things you must stay away from for the duration of your weight-losing experience. It never hurts to try new things, and on a reducing diet every new food or combination of foods you can add to your Special Diet will make your menus more varied and interesting.

Should that little demon in your mind try to defeat your diet by continuously reminding you that you "hate" certain foods, you can put a stop to it by remembering that what you really hate more than anything else is being fat.

Dinner menus are divided into three sections. The "At-Home Dinners" are informal and easy to prepare. By adding potatoes, rice or some other starch and a non-dieter's dessert, these meals will be enjoyed by the entire family and provide for their nutritional needs. The "Company Dinners" have been planned as a compliment to your guests. These meals may be served with pride and will be savored by dieters and non-dieters alike. The "Invited Out" section was designed to make accepting dinner invitations more pleasurable. It takes a bit of know-how to cope with a table that's laden with fattening foods, but once you've mastered a few of the tricks you'll be able to select without fuss or fanfare.

(*Note:* All dinners are based on the women's plan and will serve one person, unless otherwise noted, and include *all* the Special Diet Requirements of protein, carbohydrate and fruit. For men, increase protein by two ounces. Increase the recipes by multiplying ingredients by number of people the dinner is to serve.)

⇒At-Home Dinners

Take advantage of a rainy in-the-house day. Stay home and prepare a really good dinner. It will keep you occupied, out of trouble and on good terms with your bathroom scale.

Jellied Beef Bouillon
Zucchini Swordfish
French-Style String Beans
Brandied Apricots

Jellied Beef Bouillon

1 packet unflavored gelatine
¼ cup cold water
¾ cup hot beef bouillon
½ teaspoon lemon juice
Fresh parsley

⇒Soften gelatine in cold water. Dissolve in hot bouillon. Add lemon juice. Set in champagne glass. Cool and chill. Garnish with crumbled fresh parsley.

Zucchini Swordfish

6 ounces swordfish, cooked
1 package frozen zucchini
1 can mushrooms, drained
4 ounces tomatoes, canned
Celery salt
Marjoram
Garlic salt
Onion salt
Grated cheese

Cook swordfish until done and set aside. Heat zucchini until thawed; then add mushrooms, tomatoes and seasonings. Flake cooked fish and add to zucchini mixture with grated cheese. Heat.

French-Style String Beans

Bring half cup of water to boil. Cook frozen French-style string beans until just defrosted and crisp. Drain. Serve immediately with grated American cheese food sprinkled over.

Brandied Apricots

½ teaspoon brandy extract
½ cup apricot syrup
½ cup dietetic apricots

Heat extract and syrup together. Pour over apricots. Chill.

There are many rewards connected with the Special Diet, only one of which is your improved figure. The recipes for this dinner are an added bonus.

Cranberry Juice
Swordfish Diablo
Sweet and Sour Squash
Brussels Sprouts
Lemon Smash

Swordfish Diablo

8 ounces swordfish
Salt, pepper
1 tablespoon lemon juice
Dash Worcestershire sauce
1 tablespoon mustard
1 tablespoon white horseradish
Paprika

Season fish with salt and pepper. Mix together remaining ingredients (except paprika) and spread on fish. Sprinkle with paprika. Broil 10 minutes.

Sweet and Sour Squash

2 cups tomato juice
1 teaspoon cider vinegar
2 cups zucchini
1 pack artificial sweetener

Bring liquids to a boil. Turn heat down. Add thickly sliced squash and artificial sweetener. Cook until tender.

Brussels Sprouts

Cook frozen sprouts according to package directions. Or cook fresh brussels sprouts in ⅓ cup water plus 1 teaspoon lemon juice, ½ teaspoon salt and ¼ teaspoon pepper.

Lemon Smash

2 packages dietetic lemon gelatine
½ cup cold water
1½ cups hot water
1½ cups cold water
½ cup buttermilk
Grated lemon peel

Soften gelatine in ½ cup cold water in blender. Add hot water and add 1½ cups cold water and buttermilk. Let chill until syrupy—about 1½ hours. Beat in blender. Return to mold and sprinkle with grated lemon peel. Chill again.

When you're enjoying meals like this, there's little reason to even think about your weight until you step on a scale and discover that several pounds disappeared while you weren't watching.

Savory Tomato Soup
Oysters and Mushrooms en Brochette
Minted Carrots
Pineapple Fluff

Savory Tomato Soup

Heat 8 ounces tomato juice with a package of beef bouillon. Sprinkle with celery salt.

Oysters and Mushrooms en Brochette

6 ounces oysters
Whole mushrooms
Soy sauce

Marinate oysters in soy sauce for 15 minutes. Thread oysters and mushrooms on skewer. Bake at 375° for 20 minutes.

Minted Carrots

4 ounces canned carrots
1 pack artificial sweetener
½ tablespoon dried or chopped mint

Place carrots in saucepan with sweetener and heat. Drain. Add mint and mix well. Serve.

Pineapple Fluff (FOUR FRUIT SERVINGS)

2 cups canned dietetic pineapple
   slices
1 package lemon gelatine
¼ cup cold water
1½ cups boiling water
¾ cup pineapple liquid
6 tablespoons water
1 tablespoon lemon juice
⅔ cup powdered milk
1 pack artificial sweetener

Drain pineapple thoroughly, reserving liquid. Cut slices into small pieces. Soften gelatine in ¼ cup cold water. Dissolve in boiling water. Stir in ¾ cup pineapple liquid (adding cold water if necessary). Chill until syrupy. Combine 6 tablespoons water and lemon juice in small deep bowl. Sprinkle dry milk over top. Beat with rotary beater, adding sweetener until consistency of whipped cream. Fold in slightly thickened gelatine mixture. Then fold in pineapple. Pour into mold or sherbet glasses. Chill.

Never underestimate the power of chicken, particularly when it's prepared according to this sophisticated, calorie slimming recipe.

Clam Juice Stiffener
Chicken Oregano
Asparagus Parmesano
Baked Pineapple

Clam Juice Stiffener

    1 cup clam broth
    1 cup tomato juice
    ½ tablespoon lemon juice
       Dash artificial sweetener
    ½ teaspoon Worcestershire sauce
    ½ teaspoon horseradish
       Salt

≥Combine and shake.

Chicken Oregano

    10 ounces chicken breasts (raw
         weight with skin and bones)
         Garlic powder, salt, pepper to taste
     2 tablespoons lemon juice
     ½ teaspoon oregano
     ½ jar sweet roasted peppers, cut in strips
     1 pack artificial sweetener
     ½ cup tomato juice

≥Season chicken with garlic powder, salt and pepper. Marinate 1 hour with all other ingredients. Bake in marinade for 50 minutes at 350°.

Asparagus Parmesano

    1 tablespoon Parmesan cheese
    ¼ cup skim milk
    Asparagus, cooked

Melt Parmesan cheese in skim milk over low heat. Pour over fresh, cooked asparagus.

Baked Pineapple

    ¼ fresh pineapple per fruit portion
    Low-calorie raspberry soda

Marinate pineapple in soda. Bake in oven at 350° until tender.

Looks can be deceiving! This menu includes a dessert that appears to be crammed with calories, yet you may treat yourself to a large, satisfying portion.

Soup on the Rocks
Antipasto
Marinated String Beans
Maple Chiffon Mold

Soup on the Rocks

    Use old-fashioned glasses. Fill with ice cubes.
    Pour consommé or bouillon over.

Antipasto

> Lettuce
> 4 ounces cold cooked shrimp
>   (boiled in dill water)
> Few red onion rings
> 3 ounces marinated string beans
> Hot peppers
> Pimentos
> Cucumber fingers
> 1 ounce provolone cheese
> 1 teaspoon capers with juice

❧On large plate lay out cups of crisp lettuce. Place shrimp in the middle, and around them arrange the onion rings, string beans, hot peppers, pimentos, cucumbers and cheese. Sprinkle capers and juice over all.

Marinated String Beans

> 1 pound green beans
> ½ cup water
> ⅓ cup cider vinegar
> 1 teaspoon salt
> 1 clove garlic
> Small onion, cut up
> ¼ teaspoon oregano

❧Wash and snip ends off beans. Cook until just tender. Drain, reserving liquid. Add the remaining ingredients to liquid. Pour over the beans. Cover and chill overnight.

Variations:

> Carrot sticks, cauliflowerettes, cucumber fingers.

Maple Chiffon Mold

> 1 packet unflavored gelatine
> 3 packs artificial sweetener
> 2 eggs, separated
> 1½ cups skim milk
> 1 teaspoon vanilla
> ¼ teaspoon maple extract
> 6 packs artificial sweetener

Mix gelatine and 3 packs of sweetener in a small saucepan. Beat in egg yolks and milk. Cook, stirring constantly, over low heat for 5 minutes, or until gelatine dissolves and custard coats a metal spoon. Remove from heat and strain into a small bowl. Stir in vanilla and maple extract. Chill 1 hour or until mixture is as thick as an unbeaten egg white.

In a medium bowl beat egg whites until foamy and double in volume; beat in 6 packs sweetener until meringue forms soft peaks. Fold in thickened gelatine mixture until no streaks of yellow remain. Pour into a 4-cup mold. Chill. (Recipe contains the equivalent of 4 ounces protein. Reduce main course to compensate for amount eaten.)

Before you start grumbling about not liking liver, give this recipe the opportunity to change your opinion.

Jellied Appetizer Cubes
Liver and Onions and Mushrooms
Banana Chiffon Pie

Jellied Appetizer Cubes

2 packets unflavored gelatine
1 cup water
1 can (13-ounces) consommé
    Madrilene
2 teaspoons lime juice
1 can chicken broth or condensed
    chicken consommé
⅛ teaspoon salt
1½ teaspoons curry powder
    Lime wedge

Soften gelatine in water in a small pan. Place over low heat, stirring until gelatine dissolves. Pour half into each of two cake pans. Stir madrilene and lime juice into one pan and chicken consommé, salt and curry powder into the other. Chill until firm. When firm, cut into cubes with a sharp knife. Spoon madrilene in bottom of serving cups and top with cubes of the chicken gelatine. Garnish with lime wedges.

Liver and Onions and Mushrooms

    4 ounces onions
    ½ cup sliced peppers
    ½ cup sliced mushrooms
    ½ cup bouillon
       Few drops Worcestershire sauce
    8 ounces raw liver, cut in strips

Sauté onions, peppers and mushrooms in bouillon and Worcestershire. In same pan, brown liver strips quickly. Serve with vegetables on top.

Banana Chiffon Pie

    1 packet unflavored gelatine
    ¼ cup cold water
    2 eggs, separated
    2 packs artificial sweetener
    ¼ teaspoon salt
    ½ cup warm water
    1 teaspoon lemon juice
    1¼ bananas, mashed
    2 packs artificial sweetener
    1 teaspoon rum extract (optional)

Soften gelatine in cold water. In saucepan, mix egg yolks, 2 packs artificial sweetener and salt. Cook over low heat, slowly adding warm water. Cook 8 to 10 minutes over low heat, or until mixture will coat metal spoon; stir often. Add gelatine and stir until dissolved. Stir in lemon juice. Chill until slightly thickened. Fold in mashed bananas.

Beat egg whites to soft peaks. Add 2 packs artificial sweetener and rum extract. Beat egg whites until stiff. Fold banana mixture into egg whites. Pour into 8-inch pie plate or into parfait glasses. (Recipe contains the equivalent of 4 ounces protein plus 1½ fruits. Reduce main course to compensate for amount eaten.)

———————————————

Let the winds blow and snows snow, for with meals like this, come spring and your fat will have melted away like the snowman on the front lawn.

White Fish Chowder
Pepper Relish
Tutti-Fruiti Dessert

White Fish Chowder

> 3 *ounces finely chopped onion*
> 1 *vegetable bouillon cube*
> ½ *pound white fish*
> ¾ *cup water*
> *Minced sprig parsley*
> ¾ *cup skim milk*
> *Salt, pepper*

Sauté onion in small amount of bouillon. Add fish cut into 1-inch cubes. Add water and parsley. Bring to a boil. Lower heat and simmer for 5 minutes. Add milk, salt and pepper. Heat.

Pepper Relish

> 2 green peppers
> ½ head cabbage
> 1 carrot
> 1 red pepper
> 1 tablespoon salt
>   Sweetener as required
> 1½ cups cider vinegar
> 1 teaspoon dry mustard
> 1 teaspoon celery seed

Chop all vegetables. Add salt and let stand two hours. Rinse in cold water. Press out all liquid. Boil vinegar, sweetener and spices. Cool. Pour on vegetables and mix together. Put in jar and refrigerate for a few days before serving.

Tutti-Fruiti Dessert   (FOUR FRUIT SERVINGS)

> 2 packages dietetic cherry gelatine
> 1 10-ounce bottle low-calorie lemon soda
> 2 cups peach juice (add water if necessary)
> 2 cups dietetic canned peaches

Dissolve gelatine in hot soda. Add peach juice. When cool add sliced peaches.

*You can prepare this meal early in the day. Then when dinner-
time rolls around, put on a pretty hostess gown, light the candles
and enjoy a meal that allows you to forget diets, dustpans and
dishes—at least for a little while.*

Cucumber Jelly
Succulent Sea Bass
Turnip Pickle
Apricot Sponge

Cucumber Jelly

2 *medium cucumbers*
2 *teaspoons chopped onion*
1½ *cups boiling water*
1 *tablespoon cider vinegar*
1 *teaspoon salt*
1 *pack artificial sweetener*
1 *package unflavored gelatine*
½ *cup cold water*

❧Pare cucumbers and grate them. Mix with onion, boiling
water, vinegar, salt and sweetener and cook for 8 minutes. Soften
gelatine in cold water and dissolve in the hot cucumber mixture.
Pour into mold.

Succulent Sea Bass

½ pound sea bass fillet
1 tablespoon lemon juice
¾ cup water
½ teaspoon salt
¼ teaspoon curry powder
1 clove garlic, minced
¼ teaspoon black pepper
2 tablespoons chopped parsley
Lemon slices

❧Put fish into small saucepan. Combine juice, water, seasonings and 1 tablespoon parsley and pour over fish. Simmer for 30 minutes. Chill. Garnish with lemon slices and remaining parsley.

Turnip Pickle

1 turnip
1 teaspoon salt
Dash chili powder
Dash pepper
½ teaspoon ground ginger
½ cup water

❧Cut turnip into ¼-inch slices. Salt and let stand overnight. Drain, reserving liquid. Combine spices, turnip liquid and water. Mix well, add turnips, and chill for 2 weeks.

Apricot Sponge

>1 packet unflavored gelatine
>¼ cup cold water
>½ cup sieved dietetic apricots
>1 tablespoon grated lemon rind
>1 tablespoon lemon juice
>2 packs artificial sweetener
>2 egg whites

Sprinkle gelatine on cold water. Heat apricot pulp, lemon rind, juice and sweetener. Dissolve gelatine in hot mixture. Chill until thick. Whip until fluffy. Fold in stiffly beaten egg whites. Turn into mold. (Recipe contains the equivalent of one ounce of protein. Reduce main course by amount eaten.)

One of the great advantages of the Special Diet is that most menus are ideal for family meals. The skinny members may want an additional starch and a richer dessert on occasion, but from a nutritional standpoint these meals are perfectly balanced.

Hawaiian Frappé
Veal Chops Parmesan
Spinach Diablo
Raspberry Fluff

Hawaiian Frappé

>Pineapple juice, unsweetened
>Artificial sweetener, to taste

Sweeten pineapple juice to taste. Pour into ice cube tray and place in freezer. Freeze to stiff mush. Beat vigorously with fork. Serve at once.

Veal Chops Parmesan

> ½ pound veal chops (allow one
>   ounce for each bone)
> 2 ounces bouillon
> 2 ounces tomato sauce
> 2 ounces water
> 1 4-ounce can sliced mushrooms
>   Onion powder
>   Garlic powder
> 1 10-ounce package frozen French-
>   style string beans

Sear veal chops. When brown add bouillon, tomato sauce, water, mushrooms, onion powder and garlic powder. Cover and simmer on medium heat for 30 minutes. Cook French-style string beans according to package directions. Drain. Remove chops from sauce. Add beans to sauce. Sprinkle with Parmesan cheese and serve with chops.

Spinach Diablo

> 1 10-ounce package frozen
>   chopped spinach
> 3 tablespoons evaporated skim milk
> 1½ tablespoons horseradish
> ½ teaspoon salt
>   Dash pepper

Drain cooked spinach. Mix remaining ingredients with spinach. Serve.

Raspberry Fluff   (TWO MILK SERVINGS)

> 1 package dietetic raspberry gelatine
> 1 cup water
> 1 cup buttermilk
> 4 packs artificial sweetener

Dissolve gelatine in hot water. Add buttermilk and sweetener. Chill until nearly stiff. Beat with electric mixer and pour into sherbet glasses.

The recipes for this menu are real finds. They're good to look at, good to eat.

Cucumber Soup
Tuna Italiana
Cranberry Fluff

Cucumber Soup

> 1 cup buttermilk
> ½ cucumber
> ¼ teaspoon salt
> ¼ teaspoon celery seed
> ¼ onion
> Dash pepper
> Sprig of fresh dill

Liquify in blender. Chill.

Tuna Italiana

1 cup combined tomato juice and
    liquid from stewed tomatoes
4 ounces stewed tomatoes
1 clove garlic, minced
1 green pepper, diced
6 ounces tuna, drained
½ teaspoon oregano

In a skillet heat all ingredients except tuna. Cook for 20 minutes. Add tuna in chunks. (You can serve this on French-style wax beans, over bean sprouts, or by itself.)

Cranberry Fluff   (ONE AND ONE-HALF FRUIT SERVINGS)

1½ cups cranberries
¾ cup low-calorie cherry soda
1 packet unflavored gelatine
½ cup cold water
1 teaspoon grated orange rind
1 teaspoon lemon juice
  Sweetener to taste

Cook cranberries in cherry soda until skins burst. Reserve a few of these cooked berries for the garnish. Soften gelatine in cold water for 5 minutes. Mix with cranberries. Blend all together with orange rind, lemon juice and sweetener. Chill and garnish with whole cranberries.

Lobster on your budget? Why not? Think of all the money you'll save when you're able to wear those beautiful sale-priced sample dresses!

Tomato Juice Cocktail
Red Lobster
Cucumber Salad
Apple Snow

Tomato Juice Cocktail

1 cup tomato juice
Dash pepper, salt
Tabasco sauce
1 teaspoon lemon juice
Lemon wedge

≥Shake all ingredients together, except lemon wedge, and chill thoroughly before serving. Serve with lemon wedge.

Red Lobster

¼ cup green pepper, chopped
½ clove garlic
Dash paprika, salt, basil
4 ounces stewed tomatoes
6 ounces cooked lobster

≥Simmer all ingredients except lobster for 10 minutes. Add lobster and stir.

Variation:

Substitute shrimp for lobster.

Cucumber Salad

  1 cup sliced cucumbers
  ⅓ cup tarragon vinegar
  1 teaspoon salt
  ⅓ cup water
    Ground pepper
  2 teaspoons liquid sweetener

❧Combine all ingredients. Chill overnight.

Apple Snow

  1 packet unflavored gelatine
  ¼ cup cold water
  1 cup boiling water
  1 medium apple
    Dash cinnamon
    Dash nutmeg
  3 tablespoons lemon juice
  4 packs artificial sweetener
  1 egg white

❧Soften gelatine in cold water. Dissolve in boiling water. Chill. Peel and grate apple with a fine grater. Add spices, lemon juice and artificial sweetener. Combine with gelatine. Chill again until quite stiff. Beat egg white until stiff. Whip gelatine with rotary beater until foamy. Fold in egg white.

A simple recipe and a simple menu add emphasis to the exceptionally mild, delicate flavor of veal.

Apple Juice
Veal Loaf
Coffee Jelly with Whipped Topping

Veal Loaf (TWO PROTEIN SERVINGS)

1 *pound ground veal*
1 *teaspoon salt*
  Dash pepper
2 *tablespoons green pepper, chopped*
1 *tablespoon onion, chopped*
⅓ *cup tomato juice*
1 *4-ounce can sliced mushrooms*

Mix all ingredients except mushrooms. Spread in 9 × 13 pan and bake for 10 minutes in 425° oven. Broil 5 minutes. Cut in half. Cover one half with mushrooms. Pour half the sauce (recipe follows) over mushroom layer. Place second layer on top: Cover with remaining sauce. Reheat.

Sauce

1 *cup tomato juice*
¼ *teaspoon Worcestershire sauce*
1 *pack artificial sweetener*

Combine ingredients and simmer for 15 minutes.

Coffee Jelly

1 packet unflavored gelatine
2 tablespoons instant coffee
4 packs artificial sweetener
1 ¾ cups water

❧Mix gelatine, coffee and sweetener in a saucepan. Add ½ cup water. Place over low heat, stirring constantly until gelatine is dissolved. Remove from heat. Add remaining water. Chill until firm. Serve with whipped topping (recipe follows).

Whipped Topping

Chill evaporated skim milk in a glass bowl until crystals form. Add 1 teaspoon vanilla plus artificial sweetener to taste and beat with an electric or hand beater. Serve immediately. If you have some left over, you can freeze and re-beat.

Summertime is outdoor time—try your chicken broiled over the coals.

Turkish Artichoke
Barbecued Chicken
Lettuce Wedge with French Dressing
Pineapple Sherbet in Orange Cups

Turkish Artichoke

    1 artichoke
    ¼ cup chopped onion
    ½ cup bouillon
    1 teaspoon lemon juice
    1 teaspoon fresh dill

Remove outer leaves of artichoke. Snip tops with scissors. Sauté onion in bouillon. Add lemon juice and spoon over artichoke. Simmer artichoke for 45 minutes, adding boiling water if necessary. Chill. Serve cold, sprinkled with dill.

Barbecued Chicken

   10 ounces chicken (raw weight,
        including skin and bone)
   ¼ cup chicken bouillon
   ½ teaspoon Worcestershire sauce
   1 teaspoon garlic powder
   ¼ cup tomato juice
   ½ teaspoon dehydrated parsley
   1 teaspoon onion powder
   ½ teaspoon dry mustard
   1 pack artificial sweetener

Remove chicken skin and marinate chicken in remaining ingredients at room temperature for 1 hour before broiling. Broil for 15 minutes each side.

French Dressing

¼ cup tomato juice
½ teaspoon dry mustard
Dash pepper
½ teaspoon salt
½ teaspoon liquid garlic
¼ cup garlic wine vinegar
Dash celery salt
½ teaspoon liquid onion
½ teaspoon liquid sweetener

Combine all ingredients and shake.

Pineapple Sherbet in Orange Cups
(TWELVE FRUIT SERVINGS—6 PORTIONS)

2 cups buttermilk
1 6-ounce can frozen unsweetened
   concentrated pineapple juice,
   thawed
18 packs artificial sweetener
6 small oranges, peeled
6 whole strawberries, washed
   and hulled

Combine buttermilk and concentrated pineapple juice in a medium bowl. Add sweetener and beat until well blended. Pour into an ice cube tray or pan, 8 × 8 × 2. Freeze until firm. Spoon into a chilled medium-size bowl and beat quickly until fluffy smooth. Return to tray. Freeze 2 to 3 hours longer, or until firm. Separate sections of each orange slightly to form a cup. Place in dessert dishes and scoop sherbet into middle. Garnish each with a fresh strawberry.

Dining Mediterranean style adds glamour to the Special Diet. While there is nothing really foreign about this menu, the recipes are delightful low-calorie adaptations of national dishes of Italy, Spain and France. Buono appetito!

Onion Soup
Haddock de Forno
Roman Broccoli
Spanish Melon with Lime Wedge

Onion Soup

1 sliced onion
1 cup water
1 bouillon cube
Salt, pepper
Parmesan cheese

Sauté onions in a little water. Add all ingredients except cheese and simmer until flavors are blended. Spoon into soup plates. Sprinkle with a dash of Parmesan cheese.

Haddock de Forno

2 tablespoons diced onions
2 tablespoons vegetable bouillon
Dash salt, pepper
1 tablespoon grated Parmesan cheese
7 ounces raw haddock
¼ cup skim milk

(continued)

⋙Cook onions in bouillon until soft. Add salt, pepper and cheese. Put haddock in baking dish and top with onion mixture. Pour milk around fish. Bake at 350° for 30 minutes.

Variation:

Use any fish.

Roman Broccoli

Cook fresh broccoli in salted water. Drain and sprinkle with lemon juice and freshly ground pepper.

⋙————————————⋘

Dine in style on frozen fish fillets, but don't defrost them at room temperature as this causes sogginess and loss of flavor. Thaw in the refrigerator or under running water only until portions separate easily.

Waldorf Salad Gelée
Broiled Flounder with Chives
Baked Carrots
Evaporated Skim Milk Whip

Waldorf Salad Gelée

1 packet unflavored gelatine
2 teaspoons lemon juice
½ cup vegetable bouillon
½ cup diced apples
1 cup diced celery

➤Sprinkle gelatine on lemon juice. Dissolve with hot bouillon. Add remaining ingredients. Chill.

Broiled Flounder with Chives

2 ounces cottage cheese
2 tablespoons chopped chives
7 ounces flounder

➤Mix cheese and chives and spread over entire surface of fish. Broil 15 minutes.

Baked Carrots

4 ounces carrots, thinly sliced
½ cup chicken bouillon
1 small onion, grated
Dash artificial sweetener
Dash Worcestershire sauce

➤Place carrots in baking dish. Add everything else and bake at 325° for 1 hour.

Evaporated Skim Milk Whip

Punch can open and measure out 1 cup into Pyrex bowl. (This is an entire day's supply of milk.) Put in freezer until well chilled. Beat together with any flavor extract and artificial sweetener until stiff peak stage.

Here's a meal the entire family will enjoy. Of course, they can have a rich dessert while you limit yourself to melon. I won't argue that it's as good as mince pie, but the real reward is wearing a smaller size.

Tomato Juice
Roast Turkey
Baked Acorn Squash
Baked Cauliflower
Melon Ball Cooler

Roast Turkey

For easy living use a turkey roll. Using a skewer, poke holes into the roll and stuff the holes with onion powder, garlic powder and tarragon leaves. Season entire roll with salt and lots of pepper. Cook according to package directions.

Baked Acorn Squash

Cut squash into quarters. Place upside down in a pan filled ¾ high with water. Bake in a 350° oven for 30 minutes. Turn squash right side up and season with salt, pepper and artificial sweetener. Sprinkle with nutmeg. Bake for an additional 30 minutes.

Baked Cauliflower

1 medium cauliflower
1 tablespoon tomato juice
1 tablespoon Parmesan cheese, grated
1 teaspoon oregano
1 teaspoon garlic salt
   Dash seasoned pepper
   Pimento

Steam cauliflower until half done. Remove to baking dish. Pour juice over cauliflower, then sprinkle cheese and rest of ingredients over it. Bake at 350° for 15 to 20 minutes. Garnish with pimento.

Melon Ball Cooler   (SIX FRUIT SERVINGS)

1 packet unflavored gelatine
½ cup cold water
1½ cups grapefruit juice
2 packs artificial sweetener
1½ cups assorted melon balls

Soften gelatine in water. Combine juice and artificial sweetener in small saucepan and bring to a boil. Dissolve gelatine mixture with juice. Cool. Arrange melon balls in champagne glasses and pour mixture over. Chill.

No time to cook for yourself? You can prepare this dinner in a jiffy, and it's something the entire family will enjoy.

Tomato Celery Soup
Seafood Italienne
Peaches with Meringue Cookies

Tomato Celery Soup

2 cups bouillon
1 cup finely chopped celery
1 cup tomato juice
Salt, pepper

⋙Simmer all ingredients until celery is tender.

Seafood Italienne

2 ounces salmon
1 ounce American cheese
2 ounces tuna
2 ounces finely chopped onion
2 ounces tomato sauce
Celery salt
Onion salt
Paprika
Italian seasoning
Minced onion

⋙Mix all ingredients together in baking pan. Heat under broiler or bake in oven at 400° or until cheese is bubbly.

Meringue Cookies

>   2 egg whites
>   ⅓ cup skim milk powder
>   ½ teaspoon vanilla extract
>   ½ teaspoon strawberry extract
>   3 packs artificial sweetener

Beat egg whites until stiff. Add skim milk powder and mix well. Add extracts and sweetener. Spoon drop onto cookie sheet. Bake at 275° for 45 minutes. (Recipe contains the equivalent of one ounce of protein. Reduce main course to compensate for amount eaten.)

———————————

With this recipe for Brook Trout, sumptuous eating and a scrumptuous slim figure go hand in hand.

Chicken Soup with Dill
Broiled Brook Trout
Spicy Mushrooms
Carrots au Gratin
Apricot Whip

Chicken Soup with Dill

>   1 cup chicken bouillon
>   1 tablespoon dill
>   Onion salt

Heat all ingredients together over low flame.

Broiled Brook Trout

> 8 ounces trout
> ½ cup lemon juice
> Salt, pepper

❧Place fish on broiler rack. Brush each piece with ½ tablespoon lemon juice. Broil in preheated broiler, about 3 inches from flame, for 5 minutes on each side. Baste each side. Salt and pepper and serve on heated platter.

Spicy Mushrooms

> 1 pound mushrooms
> 1 clove garlic
> ½ cup water
> 1 pack instant chicken broth

❧Wash, dry, clean and slice mushrooms. Rub skillet with garlic. Combine water and broth and heat in skillet. Add mushrooms and sauté quickly until done, 4 or 5 minutes.

Carrots au Gratin

4 ounces cooked carrot slices
¼ cup bouillon
1 tablespoon dry grated cheese
Pinch thyme

Place carrots in baking dish. Pour bouillon over. Cover with cheese and add thyme. Bake uncovered at 350° for 20 to 25 minutes.

Apricot Whip   (FOUR FRUIT SERVINGS)

2 8-ounce cans dietetic apricot halves
1 package dietetic orange gelatine
1 cup boiling water
1 tablespoon lemon juice
¼ teaspoon rum extract

Drain apricots, saving liquid. Add water to make 1 cup liquid. Chop apricots and set aside. Dissolve gelatine in boiling water. Add measured liquid, lemon juice and rum extract. Chill until slightly thickened. Place in bowl of ice and water; whip with rotary beater until fluffy and thick. Fold in chopped apricots. Pour into molds and chill until firm.

When you're hungry for some "stick-to-the-ribs" food, this meal will hit the spot. Fortunately it's also right on target insofar as your diet is concerned.

Cream of Mushroom Soup
Braised Beef Cubes
Apples and Sauerkraut
French Peas
Bavarian Cream

Cream of Mushroom Soup   (TWO MILK SERVINGS)

> 2 cups skim milk
> 1 medium onion, chopped
> 1 cup mushrooms
> ¼ teaspoon salt
> ¼ teaspoon paprika

Scald milk in double boiler. Add onion, mushrooms and seasonings. Cook 20 minutes.

Braised Beef Cubes

> 8 ounces lean round of beef,
>   cut in 1½-inch cubes
> 1 onion bouillon cube
> 1 tablespoon vinegar
> 1 bay leaf
>   Salt, pepper
>   Horseradish

≥Place all ingredients except horseradish in heavy pot with tight-fitting cover. Add water to cover. Simmer over lowest possible flame until meat is tender (about 1½ hours). Add water if necessary, but there should be very little when ready to serve. Drain well and top with horseradish.

Apples and Sauerkraut

1 cup bottled or fresh sauerkraut
1 apple, thinly sliced

≥Combine sauerkraut and thinly sliced apple. Bake in 350° oven until apple is tender.

French Peas

4 lettuce leaves
3½ ounces fresh shelled peas
½ small onion, sliced
¼ teaspoon salt
2 drops artificial liquid sweetener
Dash pepper

≥Line saucepan with lettuce leaves. Place peas in pan. Spread slices of onion over peas. Sprinkle with seasonings. Cover and cook over very low heat about 10 minutes, or until peas are tender.

Bavarian Cream

1 packet unflavored gelatine
¼ cup cold water
½ cup skim milk powder
2 eggs, separated
1¾ cups boiling water
½ cup skim milk powder
½ cup ice water
1 tablespoon liquid artificial
    sweetener
1 teaspoon vanilla
1 tablespoon powdered instant coffee

Soften gelatine in cold water. Add ½ cup skim milk powder and 2 slightly beaten egg yolks. Place mixture in saucepan and add boiling water to yolk mixture. Stir until smooth. Cook over low heat, stirring constantly, until consistency of soft custard. Allow to cool and set. Beat egg whites until very stiff. Beat together ½ cup skim milk powder, ice water, liquid sweetener, vanilla and instant coffee. Fold in egg whites. Refrigerate 2 hours. (Recipe contains the equivalent of 4 ounces of protein. Reduce main course to compensate for amount eaten.)

Experimenting with foods you may never have cooked or tasted helps broaden your knowledge of the culinary arts as it narrows down your profile.

Egg and Artichoke Hearts in Aspic
Shad Roe
Squash Pancakes
Almond Gelée

Egg and Artichoke Hearts in Aspic

> ½ *packet unflavored gelatine*
> ¼ *cup cold water*
> ½ *cup hot chicken bouillon*
> 1 *teaspoon lemon juice*
> *Salt, pepper*
> 4 *ounces cooked frozen artichoke*
>   *hearts*
> 1 *egg*

Soften gelatine in cold water. Dissolve in hot bouillon. Add lemon juice, salt and pepper. Arrange artichoke hearts on bottom of flat soup plate. Poach egg and lay gently on artichokes. Cover with gelatine mixture.

Shad Roe

> 6 *ounces raw shad roe (8 ounces if*
>   *egg is omitted from previous recipe)*
> ½ *teaspoon salt*
> 1 *teaspoon vinegar*
> *Lemon juice*
> *Paprika*
> 1 *lemon slice*

(continued)

➤Parboil roe in salted and vinegared water. Simmer 10 minutes. Cool. Place in casserole and sprinkle with lemon juice and paprika. Broil until light brown. Turn and repeat. Garnish with a lemon slice.

Squash Pancakes

> 1 cup grated raw summer squash
> Salt, pepper
> 1 egg yolk

➤Mix all together. Drop by tablespoon onto heavy skillet and cook until firm on bottom. Flip and cook other side. (Recipe contains the equivalent of 1½ ounces of protein. Reduce main course to compensate for amount eaten.)

Almond Gelée

> 1 packet unflavored gelatine
> ⅓ cup cold water
> ¾ cup boiling water
> 4 packs artificial sweetener
> 1 cup skim milk
> 1 teaspoon almond extract
> Mandarin oranges

➤Soften gelatine in cold water. Add boiling water and sweetener. Stir until dissolved. Pour in milk and almond extract. Mix well. Put in small cake pan and chill. Cut into half-inch cubes and serve with mandarin oranges.

Anatole France once wrote, "A soul without love is like beef without mustard; an insipid dish." In my opinion, mustard does equally as much to heighten the enjoyment of a quick and easy chicken dish.

Cranberry Fizz
Chicken Mustard Chive
Steamed Asparagus
Mashed Carrots
French Vanilla Ice Cream

Cranberry Fizz

1 bottle low-calorie cranberry juice
1 bottle (7 ounces) carbonated water

Mix low-calorie cranberry juice and carbonated water in a pitcher. Pour over ice.

Chicken Mustard Chive

6 ounces cooked, skinned chicken
⅓ cup buttermilk
2 tablespoons prepared mustard
2 tablespoons chives
Salt, pepper to taste

Dice chicken. Heat buttermilk, mustard and chives. Add chicken and simmer about 10 minutes. Serve over asparagus.

Steamed Asparagus

Cut hard ends off asparagus. Put in skillet in small amount of water. Cook until tender.

Mashed Carrots

4 ounces raw carrots
Buttermilk
Salt, pepper to taste
Chives
Parsley

Cook carrots in jackets. Skin and put through masher or blender. Beat in enough buttermilk to moisten, adding salt and pepper. Heap in a mound and sprinkle with chives and parsley.

French Vanilla Ice Cream (FIVE MILK SERVINGS)

Step 1

2 eggs
2 cups skim milk
1 packet unflavored gelatine
¼ teaspoon salt
1½ tablespoons liquid sweetener
2 teaspoons vanilla

Place eggs, milk, unflavored gelatine, salt and liquid sweetener in blender or mixer. Mix until eggs are well blended. Then cook in top of double boiler until mixture coats metal spoon (about 5 minutes after water boils). Remove from heat and add vanilla. Cool and chill.

Step 2

> *1 cup cold water*
> *1 cup powdered skim milk*
> *1 tablespoon lemon juice*

❧In a large mixing bowl, add cold water to powdered skim milk and 1 tablespoon lemon juice. Whip in electric mixer until stiff peaks form (about 10 minutes).

When Step 1 mixture is chilled, fold into Step 2 mixture and freeze. When frozen, remove from freezer and stir with wooden spoon until ice crystals are dissolved. Re-freeze. Let set 2 hours before eating. (Recipe contains the equivalent of 4 ounces of protein. Reduce main course to compensate for amount eaten.)

Zesty seasonings add spice to the lives of dieters. Meals are never monotonous—they are always something to anticipate.

Cream of Chicken Soup
Spicy Scallops
Pepper Peas
Favorite Zucchini
Apple Compote

Cream of Chicken Soup

> *1 cup water*
> *½ cup dry milk powder*
> *1 chicken bouillon cube*
> *Onion powder*
> *Dash pepper*
> *Chopped parsley*

❧Bring everything to a boil except parsley. Simmer, blend and serve with a sprinkle of parsley.

Spicy Scallops

8 ounces scallops
1 clove garlic
2 tablespoons bouillon
Dash salt, pepper
Paprika

⇒Wash scallops thoroughly to remove sand. Mash clove of garlic into bouillon and cook 5 minutes. Toss with raw scallops. Sprinkle scallops with salt, pepper and paprika and broil 3 inches from heat for 5 minutes.

Pepper Peas

Cook frozen peas until just tender. Sprinkle with freshly ground pepper.

Favorite Zucchini

2 zucchini squash
2 cups bouillon

⇒Wash and dice zucchini. Cook zucchini in bouillon. (Do not overcook.)

Apple Compote (EIGHT FRUIT SERVINGS)

15 packs artificial sweetener
2 cups water
2 teaspoons cinnamon
8 apples, peeled and quartered

Combine sweetener, water and cinnamon in a saucepan. Boil for 15 minutes. Add the apples and cook over low heat for 10 minutes. Turn apples frequently.

———————————————

An artfully contrived dish such as Curried Cod Bake, holds great interest for those who hunger for something unique and unusually tasty.

Clam Cocktail
Curried Cod Bake
Jellied Spinach Ring
Baked Turnip
Orange Custard

Clam Cocktail

Serve icy clams on the half shell on a bed of lettuce. Serve with cocktail sauce (p. 76).

Curried Cod Bake (TWO PROTEIN SERVINGS)

                1 pound frozen cod, partly thawed
                1 large onion, chopped
                1 clove garlic, minced
                1 tablespoon water
                1 medium-size apple, pared,
                    quartered, cored and sliced
                4 ounces tomato sauce
                ½ cup water
                1 teaspoon salt
                ½ teaspoon curry powder
                  Dash pepper

Place cod in shallow baking dish. In a medium-size frying pan, sauté onions and garlic in water until soft. Stir in remaining ingredients. Heat, stirring constantly, to boiling. Spoon over fish. Cover. Bake at 350° for 1 hour, or until fish flakes easily. (Reduce protein to compensate for clams. Recipe contains ½ fruit serving each portion.)

Jellied Spinach Ring

                1 10-ounce package frozen
                    chopped spinach
             1½ cups hot spinach liquid
                1 packet unflavored gelatine
                ¼ cup cold water
                2 chicken bouillon cubes
                ½ teaspoon salt
             1½ teaspoons lemon juice
                ½ teaspoon grated onion
                6 lettuce leaves

Cook spinach as directed on package. Drain off spinach liquid into measuring cup and add enough hot water to make 1½ cups liquid. Dissolve gelatine in ¼ cup cold water in a mixing bowl. Add hot spinach liquid and bouillon cubes to gelatine. Stir until dissolved. Add spinach, salt, lemon juice and grated onion. Blend. Turn into 1-quart ring mold. Chill until firm. Unmold on lettuce.

Baked Turnip

½ pound turnip
Salt, pepper

Wash and scrub turnip. Bake at 350° for 1 hour or more. When done, cut crosswise gashes. Season to taste.

Orange Custard

1 cup water
¼ cup dry milk powder
1 egg
2 packs artificial sweetener
¼ teaspoon grated orange rind
¼ teaspoon orange extract

Pour water into top of double boiler. Sprinkle milk over and beat until blended. Scald. Beat egg until thick. Beat in sweetener, orange rind and orange extract. Gradually stir milk into egg mixture. Pour into custard cups. Put in baking pan half filled with water. Bake 45 minutes at 350°. (Recipe contains the equivalent of two ounces of protein. Reduce main course to compensate for amount eaten.)

Tender, juicy chicken basted with a zesty sauce creates a delightful flavor surprise that's as easy on your budget as it is on your figure.

Asparagus and Pimento Salad
Deviled Chicken
Dill Mushrooms
Peas and Onions
Fresh Pineapple with Mint

Asparagus and Pimento Salad

1 can asparagus (or cooked cold,
   fresh asparagus)
1 can pimento
   Lettuce
   Herbed vinegar
   Capers

➤Arrange asparagus and pimento cut in strips on bed of lettuce. Sprinkle lightly with herbed vinegar and/or capers. Chill.

Deviled Chicken

10 ounces broiling chicken
   (raw weight, including skin
   and bones)

➤Skin chicken. Marinate at room temperature for 1 hour in Devil Sauce (recipe follows). Shake off excess sauce. Broil, cut side up, 4 to 5 inches from flame. Cook slowly for 35 to 40 minutes, basting every 10 minutes.

Devil Sauce

½ cup tomato juice
1 teaspoon chili powder
Salt, pepper
¼ teaspoon dry mustard
¼ teaspoon hot pepper sauce
1 tablespoon vinegar

Mix ingredients and heat slowly until flavors mingle.

Dill Mushrooms

2 4-ounce cans mushroom caps
3 tablespoons vinegar
1 pack artificial sweetener
1 teaspoon salt
½ teaspoon dill

Pour mushrooms and liquid into a small bowl. Stir in remaining ingredients. Mix lightly and cover. Chill several hours or overnight. Drain before serving.

Peas and Onions

3 ounces frozen peas
1 ounce pearl onions
Salt, pepper

Cook peas in small amount of water. Add onions. Heat. Season with salt and pepper.

Fresh Pineapple with Mint

    1 pineapple, very ripe
    2 tablespoons mint, finely chopped
    Whole mint leaves

✺Carefully peel the pineapple. Cut it into chunks. Sprinkle with chopped mint and decorate with whole mint leaves.

⇒————————⇐

If you have a fancy mold, use it when making this Liver Loaf. Parsley makes an attractive garnish to this nutritious entrée.

Tomato Soup
Liver Loaf
Snow Peas
Whipped Cauliflower
Glazed Apples

Tomato Soup

    8 ounces tomato juice
    3 peppercorns
    Salt to taste
    ½ bay leaf
    1 tablespoon onion powder
    Artificial sweetener to taste

✺Simmer all ingredients 10 minutes. Strain into hot cups.

Liver Loaf (TWO PROTEIN SERVINGS)

1 pound beef liver, sliced
1 cup boiling water
2 vegetable bouillon cubes
1 packet unflavored gelatine
½ cup cold water
1 teaspoon salt
1 teaspoon onion juice
2 teaspoons Worcestershire sauce

Cook liver in 1 cup boiling water until tender (10 minutes). Drain well. Put liver through chopper. Place bouillon in just enough boiling water to dissolve it. Soften gelatine in ½ cup cold water. Dissolve over low heat. Combine chopped liver with bouillon and dissolved gelatine. Add salt, onion juice and Worcestershire sauce. Mix well. Pour into 2-cup loaf pan. Chill until firm. Unmold and cut into slices.

Variation:

For a different taste, try a pinch of allspice in seasonings.

Snow Peas

1 10-ounce package snow peas, frozen
1 bouillon cube
1 dash soy sauce
¼ cup mushrooms

Cook pea pods as directed on package in water to which a bouillon cube and soy sauce has been added. Garnish with mushrooms.

Whipped Cauliflower

    1 10-ounce package cauliflower
    1 cup chicken broth
    2 tablespoons skim milk
       Parsley
       Rosemary

❧Cook cauliflower in broth. Put in blender with skim milk, parsley and rosemary. Do not overblend.

Glazed Apples (SIX FRUIT SERVINGS)

    3 large baking apples
    ¾ cup dietetic ginger ale
    ½ teaspoon grated lemon rind
       Few drops red food coloring

❧Halve and core apples. Place cut side down in a shallow baking dish. Mix ginger ale, lemon rind and food coloring. Pour over apples and cover baking dish. Bake 20 minutes at 400°, basting once or twice. Uncover. Baste apples again and bake 15 minutes longer, or until tender.

Did you know that there are over two hundred species of fish? Add this to the many hundreds of ways in which they can be prepared and you'll understand why five seafood meals a week need never be boring.

Shrimp Cocktail
Halibut Creole
Tossed Green Salad
Raspberry Orange Sherbet

Shrimp Cocktail (EIGHT SERVINGS)

1 cup water
1 tablespoon vinegar
1 stalk celery leaves, chopped
1 scallion, chopped
1 bay leaf
Cayenne or hot pepper sauce
Salt to taste
Garlic salt to taste
1 pound shrimp

Boil water, vinegar, celery, scallion and seasonings together for 10 minutes. Prepare shrimp—peel, remove sand and veins, and wash. Add shrimp to stock and simmer 5 minutes. Remove, drain and chill. Serve on chopped lettuce with Tomato Hot Sauce (recipe follows). (Recipe contains the equivalent of 16 ounces of protein. Reduce the main course to compensate for amount eaten.)

Tomato Hot Sauce

1 4-ounce can tomato sauce
1 teaspoon chili powder
1 tablespoon hot cherry peppers
    (optional)

❧Combine all ingredients. Bring to a boil. Chill.

Halibut Creole

8 ounces halibut
    Salt, pepper
2 ounces thick peeled tomato
½ cup chopped green pepper
2 ounces chopped onion

❧Place fish in Teflon baking pan (or use foil lining). Sprinkle with salt and pepper. Cover with rest of ingredients. Bake 20 to 25 minutes at 400°. Baste every 10 minutes.

Tossed Green Salad

> Variety of lettuce: Boston, iceberg,
>   romaine, endive, etc.
> Garlic
> Salt
> Fresh ground pepper
> Vinegar

❧The more varieties of greens you use, the better. Buy at least three, if they are available. Wash and dry thoroughly. Tear in bite-size pieces. Put in bowl that has been rubbed with garlic. Dissolve salt and fresh ground pepper in vinegar and sprinkle over salad. Serve plain, or add the following: raw cauliflower; cucumber sticks; radish slices; raw, thinly sliced mushrooms.

Raspberry Orange Sherbet   (FOUR FRUIT SERVINGS)

> 1 cup red raspberries
> 1 cup orange juice
> 2 tablespoons lemon juice
> ¼ cup water
> 3 egg whites, beaten stiff
> 6 packs artificial sweetener

❧Blend raspberries with orange and lemon juices. Add water. Fold in egg whites. Turn into a chilled bowl and beat well with rotary or electric beater, gradually adding sweetener. Freeze until firm. (Recipe contains the equivalent of 1½ ounces of protein. Reduce the main course to compensate for amount eaten.)

Fish provides the dieting cook with an opportunity to show off her culinary ability by making a spectacular entree like these Deviled Scallops.

Oyster Cocktail
Deviled Scallops
Lettuce and Spinach Salad
Broiled Tomato
Strawberry-Rhubarb Compote

Oyster Cocktail

Cracked ice
Oysters on the half shell
Parsley
Paprika
Lemon wedges

Set cocktail glass in middle of soup plate. Fill plate with ice. Arrange oysters. Sprinkle with parsley and paprika. Garnish with lemon. Serve with cocktail sauce (p. 76). (For each 5 oysters deduct 1 ounce protein from main course.)

Deviled Scallops

6 ounces raw scallops
1½ ounces cottage cheese
¼ teaspoon prepared mustard
Salt to taste
Cayenne
Few drops Worcestershire sauce
Grated cheese (optional)

Parboil scallops in boiling water 5 minutes. Chop and set aside. Cream cottage cheese, mustard, salt and cayenne. Let stand ½ hour. Combine scallops and cottage cheese mixture. Place in baking dish, sprinkle with grated cheese (if desired) and bake 20 minutes at 375°.

Lettuce and Spinach Salad

Lettuce leaves
Fresh spinach leaves
Scallions
4 to 5 radishes

Wash lettuce and spinach carefully. Remove stem portion of spinach. If lettuce leaves are large, break into smaller sections. Slice scallions and add to spinach and lettuce. Slice radishes very thin and add to mixture. Pour evaporated skim milk dressing (recipe follows) over all and toss carefully.

Evaporated Skim Milk Dressing

Sweetener to taste
⅓ cup vinegar
½ teaspoon salt
½ cup evaporated skim milk

Combine sweetener with vinegar and salt for desired taste. Beat in milk until it thickens, or blend.

Broiled Tomato

>1 *medium tomato*
>*Salt, pepper to taste*
>¼ *teaspoon minced onion*
>1 *tablespoon grated Parmesan cheese*
>½ *teaspoon chopped parsley*

Cut tomato in half crosswise. Top with salt, pepper, onion and cheese. Broil until lightly browned. Top with parsley.

Strawberry-Rhubarb Compote
(FOUR FRUIT SERVINGS, EXCLUSIVE OF TOPPINGS)

>2 *cups rhubarb*
>½ *cup water*
>9 *packs sweetener*
>*Unsweetened pineapple juice*
>1 *pint fresh strawberries*
>1 *teaspoon lemon juice*
>¼ *teaspoon orange extract*
>⅛ *teaspoon cinnamon*

Combine rhubarb, water and sweetener in saucepan and heat to boiling point. Cover and cook over low heat about 3 minutes, or until rhubarb is tender. Drain rhubarb liquid into quart measure and add pineapple juice to make 4 cups. Saving only enough strawberries for a garnish, blend rhubarb and strawberries in electric blender or force through food mill. Blend with rhubarb liquid, lemon juice, orange extract and cinnamon. Chill. Garnish with pineapple, apple or orange topping (recipes follow).

Pineapple Topping
(ONE FRUIT SERVING AND ONE MILK SERVING)

> ⅓ cup dry milk powder
> ½ cup well-chilled, unsweetened
>   pineapple juice
> 2 tablespoons lemon juice
> 6 packs sweetener

≳Thoroughly mix dry milk and pineapple juice. Whip until soft peak stage (about 3 minutes). Add lemon juice and whip for a few more minutes, slowly adding sweetener until peaks form.

Apple Topping
(ONE FRUIT SERVING AND ONE MILK SERVING)

> ⅓ cup dry milk powder
> ½ cup well-chilled unsweetened apple juice
> 2 tablespoons lemon juice
> 6 packs sweetener

≳Proceed as for pineapple topping.

Orange Topping
(ONE FRUIT SERVING AND ONE MILK SERVING)

> ⅓ cup dry milk powder
> ½ cup well-chilled orange juice
> 2 tablespoons lemon juice
> ⅛ teaspoon mint extract
> 6 packs sweetener

≳Proceed as for pineapple topping, adding mint extract.

When feeling exotic, try this recipe. The hint of paprika and whisper of garlic that flavor this Chicken Hungarian are certain to make this one of your favorite recipes.

Cabbage Soup
Chicken Hungarian
Beans Oriental
Cold Fancy Tomatoes
Stewed Blueberries

Cabbage Soup

1 small onion, minced
1 small cabbage, grated
4 beef bouillon cubes
3 cups water
Salt, pepper to taste

Sauté onion and grated cabbage in small amount of water. Bring bouillon to boil in remaining water. Add cabbage, onion and seasonings. Simmer 10 minutes.

Chicken Hungarian   <small>(SIX PROTEIN SERVINGS)</small>

4 pounds broiling chicken
2 medium onions, diced
2 cloves garlic, crushed
1 red pepper
1 tomato, diced
  Salt to taste
8 green peppers
1 cup water
2 tablespoons paprika
½ cup bouillon

Cut chicken into pieces. Skin it and salt well. Sauté onion in bouillon until transparent. While onion is cooking, core peppers (discard seeds). Slice peppers lengthwise into ½-inch strips. When onion is transparent, add half of peppers, garlic and tomato. Sauté until peppers are soft. Add chicken. Stir in one tablespoon paprika and water. Cover. Bring to a boil, then simmer 50-60 minutes at low flame. Salt to taste and add rest of green pepper just before serving.

Beans Oriental

> 1 small onion, chopped
> 1 10-ounce package French-style string beans
> 1 1-pound can bean sprouts, drained
> 1 small can mushrooms
> 3 tablespoons soy sauce
> ½ teaspoon monosodium glutamate

❧Cook onion in Teflon pan or heavy skillet until tender. (Add 1 tablespoon water to onion if needed.) In same pan cook string beans, bean sprouts, mushrooms, soy sauce and monosodium glutamate. Simmer for 15 minutes in uncovered pan. (Recipe contains all free food except for onion which is a Limited Vegetable and could be replaced by a teaspoon of onion flakes so that recipe could be eaten at any time.)

Cold Fancy Tomatoes

> 4 ounces tomatoes
> Salt, pepper to taste
> Powdered dill
> Sour cream, Diet Workshop style
> Pinch curry
> Pinch paprika
> Chopped parsley

❧Drop tomatoes into boiling water so that skin will fall off easily. Quarter and season with salt, pepper and powdered dill. Refrigerate. Mix sour cream (p. 39) with curry and paprika. Chill. Serve dollop on tomato and top with chopped parsley.

Stewed Blueberries (FOUR FRUIT SERVINGS)

½ cup water
4 packs artificial sweetener
1 pint blueberries

➜In saucepan combine water and sweetener and bring to a boil. Add blueberries. Reduce heat and simmer 5 to 9 minutes, or until blueberries are tender. Serve warm or cold.

This colorful meal starts off with a refreshing fruit cup followed by a glamorous meatball dish made with ground veal and Chinese vegetables. For a finale, there's an applause-winning mousse.

Fruit Cup
Veal Mishmash
Orange-Coffee Mousse

Fruit Cup (FOUR FRUIT SERVINGS)

1 orange, sectioned
1 cup melon balls
12 whole strawberries
Low-calorie cream soda

➜Arrange equal portions of the fruits in 4 fruit cups. Marinate in small amount of cream soda. Chill and serve. (If you want an extra fancy touch, use a dollop of Diet Workshop sour cream [p. 39] on each serving, remembering it's part of your milk allowance.)

Veal Mishmash

1 pound ground veal
Garlic powder
1 chopped onion
1 green pepper, sliced
1 can tomato sauce
2 cans Chinese vegetables

❧Form veal into tiny balls and sear in heavy skillet with garlic powder. Add onion, green pepper, Chinese vegetables and tomato sauce and cook 1 hour. (An extra can of mushrooms and/or a package of French-style string beans can be added.)

Orange-Coffee Mousse

1 package dietetic orange gelatine
1 tablespoon skim milk powder
½ teaspoon instant coffee
Nutmeg

❧Prepare gelatine according to directions on package. When syrupy, pour into blender, adding dry milk and coffee. Run on "low" for about 10 minutes (mixture should double in blender). Pour into parfait glasses and return to refrigerator for 1 hour or more. Dust top with nutmeg.

There's no need to forego rich, creamy soups and fancy desserts on the Special Diet. Made according to these recipes, they have a wealth of flavor, yet you won't gain an ounce—in fact, they'll help you maintain a steady weight loss.

Cream of Asparagus Soup
Broiled Finnan Haddie
Broccoli Salad
Golden Carrots
Meringue Peaches

Cream of Asparagus Soup

1 10-ounce package frozen asparagus
    (or 1 pound fresh)
1 teaspoon onion flakes
    Pinch fennel
1 ½ cups water
    Liquid skim milk

Cook asparagus, reserving cooking water. Cut off tips to use later. Add stalks, onion flakes and fennel to asparagus water. Add 1½ cups water. Boil 5 minutes, then puree in blender. Add enough scalded skim milk to make 3 cups liquid in all. Cook and stir 5 minutes. Pour over asparagus tips. (Remember to deduct milk from day's allotment.)

Broiled Finnan Haddie

> 8 ounces raw finnan haddie
> 1 teaspoon lemon juice
> ½ teaspoon paprika
> 2 tablespoons chives, chopped

Broil fish until brown on both sides. Put in pan and cover with hot water. Let stand 10 minutes. Drain and cover with lemon juice, paprika and chives.

Broccoli Salad

> 1 medium bunch cold, cooked
>   broccoli
> 1 hard-boiled egg, chopped
>   Roasted sweet peppers,
>   cut in strips
>   Capers
> 1 tablespoon liquid from capers
>   Lettuce

Toss all ingredients except lettuce. Serve on lettuce bed. (Recipe contains the equivalent of 2 ounces of protein. Reduce main course to compensate for amount eaten.)

Golden Carrots
(FOUR FRUIT SERVINGS AND FOUR LIMITED VEGETABLE SERVINGS)

½ teaspoon salt
1½ cups water
2 cups sliced carrots
2 cups dietetic pineapple chunks
¼ teaspoon nutmeg

Add salt to water; add carrots and cook until tender. Drain, reserving 1 cup of the water in which the carrots were cooked. Drain pineapple chunks, reserving juice. Bring carrot and pineapple juices to boil. Add nutmeg. Combine juices with carrots and pineapple.

Meringue Peaches   (SIX FRUIT SERVINGS)

6 dietetic peach halves
1 teaspoon lemon rind
3 packs sweetener
Egg white, beaten

Drain peaches. Place 6 halves on cookie sheet, hollow side up. Sprinkle halves with lemon rind. Make a meringue of the egg white and sweetener. Spoon meringue on peach halves in peaks. Bake at 350° for 20 minutes until peaches are heated through and meringue is delicately browned.

*When you follow the Special Diet you've got nothing to lose
but excess weight. Everything from soup through dessert makes
this meal an adventure in good eating.*

Vegetable Soup
Ris de Veau
Green Spinach Torta
Lemon Lime Royale

Vegetable Soup

> 1 quart chicken consommé
> 3 cups mixed fresh vegetables
>   chopped very, very fine
> Salt, pepper to taste

❧Heat the consommé to boiling. Add the vegetables and
seasonings and continue boiling gently not more than 5 minutes.
Vegetables may be French-style string beans, radishes, cucumbers,
asparagus, broccoli, cabbage, cauliflower, celery, mushrooms,
green or red peppers, spinach, squash—with any of the
greens you choose added.

Ris de Veau

> 1 pair sweetbreads
> 4 ounces sliced onions
> 4 ounces sliced carrots
> ¾ cup chicken bouillon
> 1 bay leaf
> ¼ teaspoon thyme

Soak 1 pair of sweetbreads in ice water 1 hour. Drain. Boil in simmering salted water for 15 minutes. Cool in ice water and trim away membranes. Cook onions and carrots in ¼ cup chicken bouillon until onions and carrots are tender. Place sweetbreads on top of vegetables, add seasonings and simmer. Add remaining chicken broth, cover and place in 350° oven for 30 minutes.

Green Spinach Torta

> 1 package frozen chopped spinach
> 1 tablespoon minced white onion
> ¼ cup finely chopped celery
> 1 teaspoon shredded parsley
> ¼ teaspoon garlic powder
> ¼ cup bouillon
> 1 egg, slightly beaten
> ¼ cup Parmesan cheese
> ½ teaspoon seasoning salt
> Salt to taste
> Dash thyme
> Vinegar

Thaw spinach. Sauté onions, celery, parsley and garlic powder in bouillon until tender. Combine with spinach and stir in egg, cheese and seasonings. Bake 45 minutes at 350°. Sprinkle with vinegar before serving.

Lemon Lime Royale   (FOUR FRUIT SERVINGS)

> 2 packages dietetic lemon gelatine
> ½ cup cold water
> 1½ cups hot water
> 6 thin slices fresh lime
> 1 medium-size grapefruit
> 2 oranges

Soften gelatine in cold water. Dissolve gelatine in hot water in a medium bowl. Chill until thickened. Spoon into 4 parfait glasses, dividing evenly. Carefully stand a lime slice in center of gelatine in each glass; chill until firm. Pare grapefruit and oranges and section into small bowl; chill. When ready to serve, drain off fruit juices (save for breakfast beverage). Spoon fruits on top of gelatine, dividing evenly. Garnish with a thin orange slice, if you wish.

———————————

If you've never tried melting cottage cheese, you have a real treat in store. And this is only the beginning! Wait until you sample the other outstanding recipes for this menu.

Stuffed Mushrooms
Baked Orange Fillet of Sole
Brussels Sprouts
Baked Pear-Orange

Stuffed Mushrooms

> 1 pound fresh mushrooms
> 2 ounces chive cottage cheese
> Hickory salt

➤Remove stems from mushrooms. Stuff caps with cheese. Sprinkle with hickory salt and broil until cheese melts. (Recipe contains the equivalent of 1 ounce of protein. Reduce main course to compensate for amount eaten.)

Baked Orange Fillet of Sole
(TWO PROTEIN SERVINGS AND ONE FRUIT SERVING)

1 pound fillet of sole
1 teaspoon grated orange rind
½ teaspoon salt
⅓ cup orange juice
2 orange slices

➤Place fillets in a single layer in a shallow baking dish. Sprinkle with orange rind and salt. Pour orange juice into dish. Bake at 350°, basting once or twice with juices in dish, for 15 minutes. Garnish with orange slices.

Brussels Sprouts

4 ounces cooked brussels sprouts
½ cup tomato juice
1 bay leaf
Salt to taste
1 teaspoon caraway seeds

➤Slice sprouts lengthwise. Simmer tomato juice with remaining ingredients except sprouts for 5 minutes. Remove bay leaf. Add sprouts and heat.

Baked Pear-Orange

 4 *fresh pears*
 ¾ *cup low-calorie orange soda*
 1 *tablespoon grated orange peel*
 ½ *teaspoon nutmeg*

Arrange pears in baking dish. Cover with orange soda and bake at 325° until tender, about 20 minutes. Sprinkle with grated orange peel and nutmeg.

———————————————

Whether you think in terms of cash or calories, lavish eating doesn't necessarily call for a lavish budget. The less expensive shoulder lamb chops are ideal for this particular recipe. And if you carefully trim away all of the fat, they'll be even less costly in calories.

Consommé
Lamb Chops Oriental
Eggplant-Zucchini Casserole
Orange Cream

Consommé

Three Suggestions:

1. *Chicken bouillon with dash sherry extract and white pepper*
2. *Beef bouillon with minced onion and hickory salt*
3. *Vegetable bouillon wtih dash tomato juice, curry and lemon slice garnish*

Lamb Chops Oriental

> 10 ounces lamb chops (raw weight
>   with bone)
> 1 clove garlic, cut in half
> ¼ cup soy sauce
>   Pinch ginger
> ¼ cup water

Trim fat from chops and put chops in casserole or pan. Mix garlic, soy sauce, ginger and water. Pour over chops. Cover and let stand in refrigerator overnight. At mealtime lay chops flat on shallow baking pan. Broil 3 inches from heat for 10 minutes. Turn and broil until brown.

Eggplant-Zucchini Casserole

> ½ cup tomato juice
> 1 tablespoon onion flakes
> 1 garlic clove
> 1 bay leaf
>   Salt, pepper to taste
> 4 ounces raw eggplant, cubed
> 1 small zucchini
>   Parmesan cheese, grated

Simmer all ingredients except cheese about 10 minutes. Pour into baking dish, removing bay leaf. Top with cheese and bake in 300° oven about 10 minutes.

Orange Cream

> 1 packet unflavored gelatine
> 1 cup skim milk
> 1 egg, separated
> 1 tablespoon grated orange rind
> ⅔ cup orange juice
> 1 pack sweetener
> 1 tablespoon lemon juice
> ¼ cup chilled evaporated skim
>   milk, whipped

Sprinkle gelatine in ½ cup skim milk to soften. Scald rest of milk and stir gelatine into it until entirely dissolved. Beat egg yolk well and slowly stir gelatine mixture into it. Add orange rind and cook over hot water, stirring constantly, until mixture coats metal spoon. Remove from heat. Add orange juice, sweetener and lemon juice. Beat egg white stiff but not dry and fold into mixture. Fold in whipped evaporated skim milk. Turn into mold and chill until firm. (Recipe contains the equivalent of 2 ounces of protein. Reduce main course to compensate for amount eaten.)

The oodles of noodles in this well-seasoned chicken soup will play a delectable trick on your taste buds. Although they add the interest of the forbidden pasta, they're really tender, succulent bean sprouts.

Chicken "Noodle" Soup
Spicy Vealburgers
Dilled Carrots
Ginger Fruit Compote

Chicken "Noodle" Soup

1 *can bean sprouts*
2 *chicken bouillon cubes*
2 *cups water*
  Dash soy sauce
  Pinch curry powder

Drain bean sprouts. Place bouillon cubes in water and bring to a boil. Add bean sprouts, soy sauce and curry. Simmer about 10 minutes.

Spicy Vealburgers

8 *ounces raw ground veal*
¼ *teaspoon cumin powder*
¼ *teaspoon garlic powder*
½ *teaspoon onion salt*
  Pinch thyme
  Salt, pepper to taste
¼ *cup chicken bouillon*

Shape veal and spices into patties or balls and brown in frying pan. Cover with bouillon and simmer over low heat for 15 minutes.

Dilled Carrots

    4 ounces baby carrots
    1 cup chicken broth
    1 tablespoon vinegar
     Salt, pepper to taste
    Dill seed

Simmer carrots gently in chicken broth until tender. Sprinkle lightly with vinegar, salt, pepper and dill seed.

Ginger Fruit Compote   (SEVEN FRUIT SERVINGS)

    6 medium-size oranges
    ¼ small, ripe pineapple,
      cut lengthwise
    1 cup low-calorie ginger ale
    Mint sprigs (optional)

Pare oranges and section. Cut core from pineapple. Slice pineapple into ¼-inch thick fan-shape pieces, then pare. Place in bowl with oranges and chill until serving time. Spoon into six dessert dishes, dividing evenly. Pour ginger ale over. Garnish each with a sprig of mint, if you wish.

———————————————————

On a wintry night this hearty dinner will warm your heart with delicious thoughts of milder weather and a wild new spring wardrobe that will be sizes smaller than the clothes you're now wearing.

Spinach Soup
Frank Kabobs
Lemon Fruit Salad

Spinach Soup (ONE MILK SERVING)

> 1 *package frozen spinach*
> ¼ *cup water*
> 1½ *tablespoons minced onion*
> 1 *cup buttermilk or skim milk*
> *Salt, pepper*
> *Nutmeg*

Cook spinach in water 5 minutes. Puree in blender or or food mill. Blend with rest of ingredients. Cook over low heat for 15 minutes.

Frank Kabobs (TWO PROTEIN SERVINGS)

> 1 *pound frankfurters*
> 2 *onions*
> 6 *tomatoes*
> *Fresh or canned mushroom chunks*
> *Fresh or dietetic canned pineapple*
> *Green pepper*

Cut franks into 1-inch pieces. Cut all other ingredients into chunks. Alternate ingredients on metal skewers. Broil 3 inches from heat source, turning to brown evenly.

Lemon Fruit Salad   (TWO FRUIT SERVINGS)

1 4-ounce can dietetic mandarin
    oranges
1 package dietetic lemon gelatine
1 ounce cottage cheese
1 pack artificial sweetener
½ teaspoon vanilla
6 to 8 fresh strawberries
  Mint sprigs

Drain oranges and save liquid. Prepare gelatine according to package directions, using liquid from oranges, adding
water to make full measure. Chill. Mix cottage cheese, sweetener
and vanilla, mashing to a paste. When gelatine is syrupy, fold in
cottage cheese and the oranges. Chill. Before serving, top with
sliced strawberries and sprig of mint. (Recipe contains the
equivalent of ½ ounce of protein. Reduce main course to compensate for amount eaten.)

Tasty Ways to Serve Fish

1. Bake in cream of mushroom soup
   (see p. 118).
2. Sprinkle with soy sauce and dry salad
   dressing mix. Broil.
3. Marinate in lime, water, garlic, soy sauce,
   salt and pepper for ½ hour. Broil.
4. Marinate in salad dressing (pp. 58, 108, 139,
   172, 186) and broil.
5. Marinate in buttermilk. Broil with garlic
   powder.
6. Bake and serve with creole sauce (recipe
   follows).

Creole Sauce (FIVE LIMITED VEGETABLE SERVINGS)

1 *medium onion*
1 *medium green pepper*
1 *clove garlic, minced*
1 *8-ounce can tomato sauce*
 Dash Tabasco
1 *bay leaf*
¼ *teaspoon salt*
⅛ *teaspoon thyme*

Slowly cook onion, green pepper and garlic in a little water. Add tomato sauce and seasonings. Simmer 20 minutes, adding water if needed.

Tasty Ways to Serve Vegetables

1. *Cook in bouillon (any kind)*
2. *Puree*
3. *Marinate in pickle juice*
4. *Sprinkle with lemon juice*

⇛Company Dinners

On the Special Diet you may have company and they won't suspect that you're a selective eater. In fact, they'll never know that you're serving them a weight-reducing menu—unless you want to tell them.

Sometimes it's amusing to keep people guessing about how you can eat so well and yet manage to stay slim, but it's usually kinder to share your secret. Remember, you aren't the only one who must watch what you eat. When you listen closely to most dinner-table conversations, you discover that usually three out of four people are concerned about putting on weight. (The other one isn't talking!) When your guests realize that they may enjoy every course you serve—including dessert—without fretting over what will happen the next day when they step on their scales, I assure you they'll be most grateful.

Remember, this is a social diet. There is no reason why it should be used as an excuse for not having company. In fact, we suggest that you entertain as frequently as time and money permit—having people compliment first your figure and then your cooking is a great boost for the ego.

Appetizers that welcome your guests in a light and festive manner will be appreciated all the more when they may be enjoyed without a worry in the world about losing one's waistline.

Hors d'Oeuvres
Canapés
Dips

(Serve with Cucumber Fingers, Crisp String Beans or Cauliflowerettes)

Chive Dip

> 16 ounces cottage cheese
> 2 tablespoons skim milk
> 2 teaspoons white horseradish
> 2 tablespoons chives
> 1½ teaspoons salt
> ½ teaspoon pepper

➤Mix and serve. (Recipe contains the equivalent of 7 ounces of protein. Reduce main course to compensate for amount eaten.)

Roquefort Dip

> 8 ounces cottage cheese
> 4 tablespoons buttermilk
> Onion powder
> 1½ ounces Roquefort cheese

➤Blend all together. (Recipe contains the equivalent of 6 ounces of protein. Reduce main course to compensate for amount eaten.)

Clam Dip

> 6 ounces cottage cheese
> 1 teaspoon Worcestershire sauce
> ¼ cup buttermilk
> ½ onion, chopped
> 1 can minced clams, drained

➤Whip cottage cheese, Worcestershire sauce and buttermilk together in blender. Add onion and minced clams. (Recipe contains the equivalent of 8 ounces of protein. Reduce main course to compensate for amount eaten.)

Shrimp and Cucumber Dip

2 large cucumbers
1 small onion
1 clove garlic
2 cups cottage cheese
1 teaspoon salt
1 tablespoon tarragon vinegar
1 tablespoon prepared horseradish
8 ounces cooked shrimp, chopped

Chill all ingredients. Trim ends from both cucumbers, but peel only one of them. Cut them in half lengthwise and scoop out seeds. Cut into pieces and blend with onion and garlic. Add cottage cheese and blend until smooth. Remove to a chilled bowl. Stir in salt, vinegar, horseradish and shrimp. Makes about 5 cups. (Recipe contains the equivalent of 14 ounces of protein. Reduce main course to compensate for amount eaten.)

Eggplant Caviar

1 eggplant
2 chopped onions
   Minced garlic
1 ripe tomato, diced
   Tarragon vinegar
   Salt, pepper
   Water

Bake eggplant until soft. Mash pulp, mix with onions and garlic. Add tomato and season to taste with salt, pepper, vinegar and water. Chill and serve on cucumber rounds.

Cucumber Rounds

Wash cucumber thoroughly. Take sharp fork
and scratch it from top to tip. Slice in ¼-inch
pieces. Place in refrigerator in salt water for
extra crispness.

Pickled Eggs

2 cups white vinegar
1 medium-size onion, sliced
    and peeled
1 teaspoon salt
    Artificial sweetener
12 hard-boiled eggs

Simmer all ingredients (except eggs) for 10 minutes.
Place eggs in glass jar. Strain mixture over. Cover and chill.
(Recipe contains the equivalent of 24 ounces of protein. Reduce
main course to compensate for amount eaten.)

Skewer Together on Sandwich Picks

1. Apples and cheese (dip apples in orange juice
   to prevent darkening)
2. Cheese, pickles and onions
3. Cucumbers and ice cold shrimp (dice cucumbers and sprinkle with seasoned salt)

➔Broil on Skewers

1. Chicken livers (*marinated in soy sauce*)
2. Frankfurter pieces and mushrooms
3. Cooked shrimp and dietetic pineapple chunks

➔Broil in Mushroom Caps

1. Ground veal mixed with onion powder, salt and pepper
2. Cottage cheese mixed with seasoned salt
3. Ground veal mixed with mozzarella cheese, garlic and oregano
4. Small pieces of Cheddar cheese

➔Cold Spreads

1. Mix together equal amounts of crabmeat and chopped dill pickle. Bind with mustard and pickle juice. Roll in cabbage leaves, which have been softened in hot water for 10 minutes.
2. Spread cottage cheese mixed with horseradish on a very thin slice of roast beef. Roll up. Chill. Cut in half and fasten with a toothpick.
3. Mix together mashed hard-boiled eggs with capers and diced dill pickles. Stuff in celery stalks.

Pickled Mushrooms

> 1 cup cider vinegar
> 2 4-ounce cans button mushrooms
> 1 pack artificial sweetener
> 1 clove garlic, minced
> 1 teaspoon salt
> 3 whole peppercorns

Combine vinegar with mushroom liquid and boil 3 to 4 minutes. Add sweetener, spices and mushrooms. Let stand overnight. Drain and serve on picks.

Radish Roses

To form petal, cut thin strips of the red peel of radishes down to stem. Place in ice water until the petals curl back.

Cucumber Fingers

Peel cucumber and cut in eighths. Sprinkle heavily with garlic and pepper.

Your fame as a hostess is practically guaranteed after your guests discover that the meal they have complimented so highly was so low in calories.

Pea Soup
Sea Kabobs
Celery and Lettuce Salad
Key Lime Mold

Pea Soup   (FOUR LIMITED VEGETABLE SERVINGS)

5 cups water
1 medium onion, sliced
1 medium carrot, sliced
1 package frozen peas
3 chicken bouillon cubes
1 teaspoon salt
Generous dash black or
cayenne pepper
1 teaspoon curry powder
Sliced mushrooms

Heat water, onion, carrot, peas, bouillon cubes, salt and pepper. Bring to a boil; then cover and simmer gently for 50 minutes, or until peas are very soft. Stir in curry. Blend mixture or put through a sieve or food mill. Return puree to saucepan. Serve topped with mushroom slices.

Sea Kabobs
(SIX PROTEIN SERVINGS AND SIX LIMITED VEGETABLE SERVINGS)

1 clove garlic, minced
¼ cup water
6 tablespoons fresh, frozen or
    canned lemon juice
1 pack sweetener
4 teaspoons salt
¼ teaspoon pepper
¼ teaspoon tabasco
½ teaspoon dried thyme
1½ pounds scallops
1½ pounds deveined, shelled
    large raw shrimp
1 can white onions
6 small tomatoes, halved
    lengthwise
2 green peppers, cut into
    2-inch squares

Sauté garlic in water for a few minutes. Stir in lemon juice, sweetener, salt, pepper, tabasco and thyme. Cool and pour over scallops and shrimp. On 6 skewers about 12 inches long arrange onions, shrimp, scallops, tomatoes and green peppers. Brush generously with sauce. Broil kabobs, turning skewers as necessary and basting often with sauce until all is golden and shrimp and scallops are done. Slip food off skewers onto guests' plates with remaining sauce.

Celery and Lettuce Salad

    1 head iceberg lettuce
    1 head romaine lettuce
    3 stalks celery, diced

Wash all ingredients and break into pieces. Place in terry towel until ready to serve. (Dressing recipe follows.)

Dressing

    1 cup wine vinegar
    1 cup water
    ½ teaspoon sweet basil
    1 cup tomato juice
    1 teaspoon seasoned pepper
    1 tablespoon chopped capers

Blend all ingredients together except capers. Add capers. Refrigerate in jar. Shake before serving.

Key Lime Mold (SIX FRUIT SERVINGS)

    1 package dietetic lemon gelatine
    1 package dietetic lime gelatine
    1 cup hot water
    1 cup cold water
    3 ounces farmer cheese
    1 cup buttermilk
    1 can dietetic crushed pineapple

Dissolve gelatine in hot water and add cold water. Blend cheese and buttermilk. Add to gelatine. Add pineapple and juice. Chill (Recipe contains the equivalent of 2 ounces of protein. Reduce main course to compensate for amount eaten.)

Remember way back when your guests left the dinner table moaning that they wouldn't be able to eat for a week? That was no compliment, lady. It was a lament. How much kinder it is to serve a meal such as this that may be enjoyed with no regrets.

Tomato Beef Bouillon
Shish Kabob
Large Tossed Salad
Blue Cheese Dressing
Frozen Orange Dessert

Tomato Beef Bouillon

Tomato juice
Beef bouillon cube

➤Heat beef bouillon cube in tomato juice until dissolved.

Shish Kabob
(SIX PROTEIN SERVINGS AND SIX LIMITED VEGETABLE SERVINGS)

3 pounds leg of lamb, cubed
4 large onions, diced
2 teaspoons oregano
2 tablespoons salt
1 teaspoon black pepper
⅔ cup soy sauce
12 large mushroom caps
12 small onions
3 green peppers, cut up

➤Place meat in bowl with the diced onions. Sprinkle with oregano, salt and pepper. Pour soy sauce over. Marinate several hours, turning occasionally. Remove meat and thread on skewers, alternating with mushrooms, onions and peppers. Brush with marinade. Broil.

Blue Cheese Dressing

    1 cup chilled buttermilk
1½ tablespoons lemon juice
1½ teaspoons liquid sweetener
   ½ teaspoon dry mustard
   ¼ teaspoon salt
   1 ounce blue cheese

Combine all ingredients and beat well. Toss with favorite greens. (Recipe contains the equivalent of 1 ounce of protein. Reduce main course to compensate for amount eaten.)

Frozen Orange Dessert
(ONE MILK SERVING AND ONE FRUIT SERVING)

   ⅓ cup nonfat dry milk
   ½ cup ice water
   ½ cup unsweetened orange
       juice concentrate
   1 teaspoon liquid sweetener
   ½ teaspoon grated orange peel

In small mixing bowl, combine dry milk and water. Beat in electric mixer at high speed until stiff peaks form. Combine orange juice and sweetener. Blend into whipped mixture at low speed. Spoon into freezer tray. Sprinkle with grated orange peel. Freeze.

If it is true that "The discovery of a new dish does more for the happiness of mankind than the discovery of a new star," try this for a shining result.

Lobster Fra Diavalo
Spring Salad
Apple Delight

Lobster Fra Diavalo
(FOUR PROTEIN SERVINGS AND FOUR LIMITED VEGETABLE SERVINGS)

4 lobsters
2 cloves garlic
¼ cup chicken broth
4 tomatoes
3 tablespoons chopped parsley
½ teaspoon salt
½ teaspoon oregano
¼ teaspoon sweet basil
⅛ teaspoon pepper
¼ teaspoon crushed red
      pepper flakes

Boil lobsters for 10 minutes. Split in half. Remove intestinal vein and roe. Crack claws. Put into baking dish, cut side down. Sauté garlic in chicken broth. Add other ingredients. Pour over lobster. Bake 10 minutes at 350°.

Spring Salad

    1 packet unflavored gelatine
    ¼ cup cold water
    1¼ cups hot water
    ¼ cup lemon juice
    3 packs artificial sweetener
    1 teaspoon salt
    1 teaspoon vinegar
    1 cup diced cucumber
    1 cup sliced radishes
    ½ cup sliced scallions
      Watercress

❧Sprinkle gelatine on cold water; dissolve in hot water. Stir in lemon juice, sweetener, salt and vinegar. Chill until syrupy. Fold in vegetables. Chill until firm.

Apple Delight
(SIX FRUIT SERVINGS AND ONE MILK SERVING)

    6 apples
    1 teaspoon unflavored gelatine
    ½ cup cold water
    1 teaspoon maple extract
    4 packs artificial sweetener
    1 cup warm liquid skim milk
      Grated rind of 2 oranges
      Juice of 4 oranges (2 cups)
    3 egg whites

❧Peel, core and grate apples. Dissolve gelatine in water. Add maple extract and artificial sweetener to gelatine. Add orange rind to milk and gradually stir in juice of oranges. Beat egg whites until stiff; fold into grated apples. Add milk mixture, fold lightly. Pour into sherbet glasses and chill. (Recipe contains the equivalent of 1½ ounces of protein. Reduce main course to compensate for amount eaten.)

———————————————

Whether your guests are dieting or not, a tender steak is certain to please everyone, especially when it's followed by a beautiful dessert that may be enjoyed without any feeling of guilt.

Grapefruit Foam Cocktail
Oriental Steak Broil
Mashed Turnip
Rainbow Cake

Grapefruit Foam Cocktail   (FOUR FRUIT SERVINGS)

> 1 egg white
> 2 cups unsweetened grapefruit juice
> 2 packs artificial sweetener
>   Nutmeg

❧Beat egg white until stiff. Combine grapefruit juice and sweetener. Fold in egg white. Pour into small glasses. Top with dash of nutmeg.

Oriental Steak Broil   (FOUR PROTEIN SERVINGS)

> 2 pounds flank or shoulder steak
> 3 tablespoons lemon juice
> 1 tablespoon soy sauce
> 1 teaspoon garlic powder
> 1½ teaspoons salt
> ⅛ teaspoon pepper

❧Pierce steak all over with a fork. Place in flat pan. Combine other ingredients in a cup and then pour over steak. Marinate steak 2 hours in refrigerator. Broil. Carve flank steak diagonally.

Mashed Turnip

> 4 ounces turnip
> Salt, pepper
> Chili powder

→Wash and pare turnip. Slice. Cook until tender in boiling salted water (5 minutes). Drain off liquid. Mash. Heat with salt, pepper and chili powder over low flame.

Rainbow Cake

> 1 package each of the following
>   dietetic gelatines:
>   Cherry
>   Lime
>   Orange
>   Lemon
>   Raspberry or strawberry
> 5 cups boiling water
> 2½ cups cold water

→Dissolve each package of gelatine separately in 1 cup boiling water. Add ½ cup cold water to each. Chill each until very thick. Whip cherry gelatine until fluffy. Spoon into 9- or 10-inch spring form pan. Chill until set but not firm. Whip and layer the remaining flavors one at a time, letting each chill until set but not firm before adding next layer. Chill until firm. Remove from pan. Serve with topping (recipe follows).

Topping

½ *cup cold water*
1 *teaspoon vanilla*
Sweetener to taste
⅔ *cup skim milk powder*

Pour ½ cup cold water in chilled mixing bowl. Add vanilla, sweetener and powdered milk. Beat at high speed for 8 to 10 minutes, or until consistency of whipped cream. Spread over top and sides of "cake."

Put on your slinkiest Mandarin hostess gown, and as guests praise the artful way you have prepared this Chinese dinner, you may also glory in their admiration of your slimmer figure.

Egg Drop Soup
Chinese Beef Ribs
Dilly Bean Sprouts
Bamboo Shoots and Pea Pods
Pineapple-Lime Parfait

Egg Drop Soup

2 *cans (14-ounces each) chicken broth*
1 *egg, slightly beaten*
2 *tablespoons chopped parsley*

Heat chicken broth just to boiling. Pour in beaten egg very slowly, stirring constantly, until egg cooks and separates into shreds. Ladle into heated cups and sprinkle with parsley. (Recipe contains the equivalent of 2 ounces of protein. Reduce main course to compensate for amount eaten.)

Chinese Beef Ribs
(SIX PROTEIN SERVINGS AND TWO FRUIT SERVINGS)

6 pounds beef or lamb ribs
Red food color
1 large bottle soy sauce
16 packs artificial sweetener
1 can dietetic apple sauce
Garlic powder
Salt

Wash ribs. Cut apart and place in roasting pan. Color ribs by painting with red food color—use your fingers. Mix together all other ingredients. Marinate for 4 hours. Bake at 325° for 1½ hours.

Dilly Bean Sprouts

1 1-pound can bean sprouts
1 cup dill pickle juice
½ cup chopped dill pickles
Red pepper rings (optional)

Drain and rinse bean sprouts. Marinate in pickle juice overnight. Serve chilled, tossed with chopped pickles and garnished with red pepper rings.

Bamboo Shoots and Pea Pods

     2 5-ounce cans bamboo shoots
     1 pound fresh or 10-ounce package
          frozen pea pods
     ½ cup bouillon
     2 tablespoons soy sauce
     1 teaspoon ginger
     1 teaspoon garlic powder

Sauté pea pods and bamboo shoots quickly in bouillon. Add soy sauce, ginger and garlic.

Pineapple-Lime Parfait   (FOUR FRUIT SERVINGS)

     3 packages lime gelatine
     1 cup boiling water
     1 cup dietetic pineapple
          crush
     1 tablespoon lemon juice
     3 tablespoons ice cold water
     3 tablespoons dry milk

Dissolve the gelatine in boiling water. Drain crushed pineapple, reserving the juice. Refrigerate crushed pineapple. Add lemon juice to pineapple juice; add enough cold water to make 1 cup liquid. Add to gelatine and chill until gelatine begins to thicken. Fold the drained pineapple into about two-thirds of the gelatine. Divide into 6 parfait glasses.

Beat the remaining gelatine until light. Whip the ice-cold water and the dry milk together until fluffy and fold into the whipped gelatine. Pile on top of the parfait glasses. Chill.

Deck the halls and invite friends to share a bountiful holiday feast that may be enjoyed without fear of putting on weight.

Artichokes Vinaigrette
Roast Turkey
Cranberry Sauce
Broccoli (p. 110)
Acorn Squash
Broken Glass Torte

Artichokes Vinaigrette

6 *artichokes*
1 *thick lemon slice*
1 *small garlic clove*
½ *teaspoon salt*
Boiling water

❧Stand 6 artichokes upright in deep saucepan just large enough to hold them snugly. Add lemon slice, garlic clove, salt and water. Boil gently, covered, 20 to 45 minutes, or until a leaf can be pulled easily from stalk. Drain artichokes upside down. Serve with vinaigrette sauce (recipe follows).

Vinaigrette Sauce

¼ cup tarragon vinegar
¼ cup water
¼ teaspoon dry mustard
1 teaspoon parsley
1 tablespoon chopped capers
1 tablespoon chopped dill pickles
½ teaspoon salt
  Freshly ground pepper

≥Mix all ingredients together. Serve as a dip with the artichokes.

Roast Turkey

1 15-pound turkey
  Onion powder to taste
  Garlic powder to taste
  Salt, pepper to taste
  Paprika to taste
1 whole onion
¼ cup soy sauce

≥Wash turkey inside and out. Season well. Place whole onion inside. Sprinkle soy sauce all over. Bake at 325° for 4 hours, or until tender.

Cranberry Sauce   (FOUR FRUIT SERVINGS)

>   4 cups cranberries
> 1½ cups water
>   16 packs sweetener
>   2 packets unflavored gelatine
>   ½ cup cold water

Cook cranberries in water until skins pop. Remove from heat; stir in sweetener. Soften gelatine in cold water. Add hot cranberry mixture and stir until gelatine dissolves. Chill. (This will not jell.)

Acorn Squash   (SIX LIMITED VEGETABLE SERVINGS)

>   3 acorn squash, halved
>   ½ teaspoon lemon juice
>   Few drops liquid sweetener
>   Cinnamon
>   Salt, pepper

Scoop out center of squash (seeds) and discard. Bake for 30 minutes at 325°, cut side down. Turn over. Season and bake again for 30 minutes.

Broken Glass Torte

(TWO FRUIT SERVINGS AND ONE MILK SERVING)

3 packages dietetic gelatine
 (different colors)
3 cups boiling water
1½ cups cold water
1 cup unsweetened pineapple juice
1 packet unflavored gelatine
½ cup cold water
1 teaspoon lemon juice
⅓ cup dry milk powder

➤Prepare 3 packs of gelatine separately, using 1 cup hot water and ½ cup cold water for each. Pour into separate ice cube trays until set.

Heat pineapple juice with gelatine and chill until syrupy. Pour ½ cup cold water into large mixing bowl. Add lemon juice and dry milk powder. Beat 8 to 10 minutes at high speed. Combine with syrupy mix and beat until blended. Cube three trays of gelatine and fold into pineapple mixture (leave a few cubes to garnish top). Pour into spring form, garnish with leftover cubes and return to refrigerator.

The appetites of your guests will be intrigued by the foreign flavor of the interesting foods on this menu.

Gazpacho
Bengalese Haddock
Carrots Piquant
Cantaloupe Salad with Dressing
Company Pie

Gazpacho   (FIVE LIMITED VEGETABLE SERVINGS)

1 clove garlic, minced
1 large can whole tomatoes
¼ cup minced green pepper
1 minced onion
2 cucumbers, thickly sliced
      (washed, not peeled)
1 tablespoon wine vinegar
Salt, pepper to taste
Lime slices

Place all ingredients except lime slices in blender and blend until mixture is smooth. Chill. Serve in individual mugs over ice cubes. Garnish with lime.

Bengalese Haddock
(FOUR MILK SERVINGS AND FOUR PROTEIN SERVINGS)

> 1 quart buttermilk
> 1 tablespoon lemon juice
> 1½ teaspoons salt
> ¾ teaspoon tabasco
> 1 tablespoon cumin seeds
> ¼ cup chopped green pepper
> 2 teaspoons turmeric
> 2 pounds haddock fillets

Combine buttermilk, lemon juice, salt and tabasco in large skillet. Bring to a boil and simmer 10 minutes. Add cumin seeds and green pepper. Sprinkle turmeric over fish fillets and rub in gently. Add fillets to buttermilk mixture and simmer 10 to 12 minutes, or until fish flakes easily with a fork.

Carrots Piquant

> 4 ounces carrots
> ½ cup tomato juice
> Dash hot pepper sauce
> Onion powder

Slimmer thinly-sliced carrots in rest of ingredients until tender.

Cantaloupe Salad

> 1 packet unflavored gelatine
> 1 tablespoon cold water
> 2 tablespoons boiling water
> 1 pint low-calorie ginger ale
> 1 pack artificial sweetener
> 1½ cups cantaloupe balls
> Chicory

≥Sprinkle gelatine in cold water. Add boiling water and stir until dissolved. Add ginger ale and sweetener. Chill until syrupy. Fold in cantaloupe balls. Pour into individual molds and chill until firm. Garnish with chicory. Serve with dressing (recipe follows).

Dressing

> ¼ teaspoon dry mustard
> ¼ teaspoon paprika
> ¼ teaspoon salt
> ¾ cup water
> 2 tablespoons vinegar
> Juice of ½ lemon, strained
> ¾ teaspoon Worcestershire sauce
> ½ cup orange juice
> ½ package artificial sweetener
> 1 clove garlic

≥Combine mustard, paprika and salt. Add remaining ingredients except garlic. Mix well and pour into container. Drop in peeled garlic clove. Cover tightly. Store in refrigerator. Shake well each time used.

Company Pie (TWO FRUIT SERVINGS)

Shell:

> 2 egg whites
> 2 packs artificial sweetener
> ½ cup dry milk powder
> 1 teaspoon vanilla extract
> 1 teaspoon lemon extract

Beat egg whites until frothy. Gradually add remaining ingredients and beat until stiff. Place in 9-inch pie plate or 9 × 9 pan, spreading evenly with knife. Bake at 275° for 50 minutes. Cool.

Filling:

> 6 ounces cottage cheese
> 1 cup dietetic peaches

Mash cottage cheese and spread evenly in baked shell. Cover with peaches.

Glaze:

> 1 package dietetic cherry gelatine
> 1 cup hot water
> ½ cup cold water
> 1 teaspoon lemon juice

Dissolve gelatine in hot water. Add cold water and lemon juice. When slightly cool, pour over pie. Chill. (This recipe contains the equivalent of 4 ounces of protein. Reduce main course to compensate for amount eaten.)

Polish up the silver and get out your finest linen table cloth—
this dinner deserves to be served in the most elegant manner.

Tomato Juice Frappé
Sirloin Roast
Celery Creole
Mint Peas
Rhubarb-Strawberry Bavarian

Tomato Juice Frappé

Tomato juice
Salt
Pepper
Worcestershire sauce
Prepared horseradish
Sweetener

❧Season tomato juice to taste with salt, pepper, Worcestershire sauce, prepared horseradish and sweetener. Pour into refrigerator freezing tray and freeze to stiff mush. Beat vigorously with fork. Serve at once.

Sirloin Roast

❧Roast meat according to your favorite recipe.

Celery Creole

2 cups celery, sliced
1 tomato, chopped
1 green pepper, chopped
1 clove garlic, minced
  Small onion, chopped
1 bay leaf
⅛ teaspoon basil
  Dash tabasco
⅛ teaspoon thyme
1 chicken bouillon cube
¼ teaspoon chili powder

Combine all ingredients and simmer for 20 minutes.

Mint Peas

4 ounces frozen peas
3 tablespoons chopped mint leaves

Cook frozen peas according to package directions. Add mint leaves just before serving.

Rhubarb-Strawberry Bavarian (FOUR FRUIT SERVINGS)

    1 pound rhubarb, cut in
        1-inch pieces
    ¼ cup water
    3 tablespoons liquid sweetener
    2 packets unflavored gelatine
    ½ cup cold water
    2 cups crushed strawberries
    ¼ cup milk powder
    ¼ cup ice water

Simmer rhubarb, water and sweetener for 15 minutes or until rhubarb is very tender. Soften gelatine in cold water for 2 minutes and add to rhubarb, stirring mixture to dissolve gelatine. Add strawberries. Chill until syrupy. Beat milk powder and ice water until soft peaks form and fold into thickened gelatine. Spoon into mold. Chill.

———————————————

After serving this meal you may find it difficult to convince anyone that you're dieting and so are they when they eat in your home—so don't even try.

Oysters on the Half Shell
Roast Lamb
Oriental Asparagus
Carrots Vichy
Braised Celery
Strawberry Chiffon Pie

Oysters on the Half Shell

    6 oysters per person
    Cracked ice
    Cocktail sauce
    Lemon wedge

≫Serve oysters (or clams on the deep halves of the shells. Allow 6 each. Arrange on ice in individual shallow bowls. Serve with cocktail sauce (recipe follows) and lemon wedge. (This recipe contains the equivalent of 2 ounces of protein. Reduce the main course to compensate for amount eaten.)

Cocktail Sauce

½ cup tomato sauce
1 tablespoon horseradish
2 teaspoons lemon juice
1 drop tabasco sauce

≫Combine all ingredients and chill.

Roast Lamb

1 leg of lamb (4 to 6 pounds),
    boned and rolled
Garlic
Salt
Parsley leaves
⅓ cup water
1 teaspoon thyme
½ teaspoon basil
1 teaspoon salt
½ teaspoon pepper

≫Make slits in meat and insert slivers of garlic, salt and parsley leaves. Place lamb in roasting pan with water. Bake 3 hours at 300°.

Mix together thyme, basil, salt and pepper. Spread over lamb and bake 30 minutes more. Add more water when necessary. Slice meat and arrange sauce on top.

Oriental Asparagus

    1 pound asparagus
    Water
    1 teaspoon soy sauce
    ½ teaspoon monosodium glutamate

➤Slice asparagus diagonally in ¼-inch slices. Place in large skillet with water to just cover bottom of skillet. Add soy sauce and monosodium glutamate. Cook over low heat until barely tender—don't overcook. Stir occasionally. (Takes about 5 to 7 minutes.)

Carrots Vichy   (FOUR LIMITED VEGETABLE SERVINGS)

    1 pound carrots, pared
    ½ cup water
    1 pack artificial sweetener
    ½ teaspoon salt
    Dash coarse black pepper
    ¼ cup chopped parsley
    Juice of 1 lemon

➤Cut carrots crosswise on an angle into very thin slices. Add water, sweetener, salt, pepper to the carrot slices. Cook, covered, over low heat until carrots are tender (about 10 minutes). Toss lightly with parsley and lemon juice.

Braised Celery

    Bunch celery
    1 teaspoon onion flakes
    Salt
    Beef bouillon
    1 tablespoon grated Parmesan
        cheese

Wash celery. Cut off leaves. Split stalks in half or cut in even lengths. Put in skillet. Add onion flakes, salt and just enough bouillon to keep celery from burning. Cover and cook until tender (15 to 20 minutes). Sprinkle with cheese.

Strawberry Chiffon Pie
(TWO FRUIT SERVINGS AND TWO MILK SERVINGS)

Crust:

> 2 egg whites
> 4 tablespoons powdered skim milk
> ½ teaspoon vanilla
> Pinch salt
> 3 packs artificial sweetener

Beat egg whites until foamy. Add remaining ingredients gradually and beat until egg whites are stiff. Spread in 9-inch pie plate. Bake at 275° for 50 minutes.

Filling:

> 3 packages dietetic strawberry
>   gelatine
> 2 cups hot water
> 2 cups cold water
> 1 cup evaporated skim milk
> 1 cup unsweetened pineapple juice

Pour 3 packages gelatine in bowl. Add hot water to dissolve. Add ice water. Chill. Put milk in freezer until crystallized. Whip crystallized milk until soft peak stage. Add pineapple juice. Whip gelatine. Fold in milk and juice mixture. Spread in shell. Chill. (This recipe contains the equivalent of 1 ounce of protein. Reduce main course to compensate for amount eaten.)

A chicken in every pot? No, but why not a hen in every plate?

Jellied Madrilene
Rock Cornish Hen
Zucchini Neapolitan
Strawberry Parfait

Jellied Madrilene

    1 *packet unflavored gelatine*
 2½ *cups water*
    3 *beef bouillon cubes*
    1 *medium tomato, cut up*
 1½ *tablespoons tomato sauce*
    2 *tablespoons tarragon vinegar*
  ½ *bay leaf*
    3 *peppercorns*
  ½ *teaspoon salt*

Sprinkle gelatine over ½ cup water to soften. Combine remaining water and ingredients and heat to boiling, stirring constantly. Remove from heat and add softened gelatine. Stir until dissolved. Strain. Chill until firm.

Rock Cornish Hen

6 Rock Cornish hens
Salt, Pepper
Garlic powder
Soy sauce

⟩Season hens with salt, pepper and garlic powder. Brush with soy sauce. Place on rack in roasting pan with water in the bottom for basting. Put into 450° oven and roast 20 minutes, basting occasionally. Add more water if necessary. Reduce heat to 350° and roast 40 minutes longer, basting occasionally.

Zucchini Neapolitan
(EIGHT LIMITED VEGETABLE SERVINGS)

2 pounds small zucchini
¼ cup chopped onions
¼ cup water
4 tomatoes
½ teaspoon salt
¼ teaspoon oregano
Pepper
2 tablespoons chopped parsley
2 tablespoons grated Parmesan
cheese

⟩Wash and cut ends from zucchini. Cut crosswise into ½-inch slices. Sauté onion in water until tender. Add tomatoes that have been peeled and quartered. Cook for 5 minutes. Add zucchini, salt, oregano and pepper and cook covered for 10 minutes. When ready to serve sprinkle with parsley and cheese.

Strawberry Parfait

(EIGHT FRUIT SERVINGS AND THREE MILK SERVINGS)

> 1½ packets unflavored gelatine
> ⅓ cup cold water
> 3 cups skim milk
> 4 eggs, well beaten
> 2 tablespoons liquid sweetener
> ½ teaspoon vanilla extract
> ½ teaspoon almond extract
> 2 cups unsweetened sliced
>   strawberries
> 2 cups orange sections

Soften gelatine in cold water. In top of double boiler, combine skim milk, eggs and ½ the sweetener. Cook over hot water until mixture coats metal spoon. Remove from heat. Blend in softened gelatine, vanilla and almond extract and stir to dissolve gelatine. Pour into 8-inch square pan. Chill until set, then cut into ½-inch cubes. Puree the strawberries with remaining sweetener. Pour over orange sections and alternate gelatine cubes in parfait glasses. (Recipe contains the equivalent of 8 ounces of protein. Reduce main course to compensate for amount eaten.)

Invited Out?

When you're going to a friend's house for dinner, be a thoughtful guest—ask if you may bring something for dessert. Make a batch of Baked Apples or a Lemon Smash. You'll be a sought-after guest and, better yet, you will know that there is something legal and palatable waiting for you at the end of the meal. Make more than would seem necessary, for these "diet" foods are inevitable scene stealers.

Don't be self-conscious about refusing certain foods and second helpings. No lengthy excuses are necessary. Just smile and say, "No thank you." The considerate hostess will understand. Of course, if you have an opportunity to mention your diet to your hostess before dinner to request her cooperation, so much the better. Otherwise, eat slowly. If there is something on your plate that you can't eat, pretend to eat it—push it around your plate as your children do.

Plan to arrive late (after the cocktail hour). If it's still in progress when you get there, be firm. Have a low-calorie soda or fruit juice, or if nothing else that is permissible on your diet is available, a glass of water. And whatever you do, keep away from the hors d'oeuvres—unless there is a bowl of raw vegetables.

Don't arrive ravenous; eat before you go. Then don't be intimidated by anyone who insists that you eat more than you know you should have. Think of the slim guests you've met at other dinner parties. Remember how you envied their disinterested look when they refused food that was being offered to them. Now it's your turn to appear ethereal—mysterious—above such mundane things as the need for food.

Keep your goal in mind. You can't afford to forget your diet for one night, one hour or one minute if you wish to lose weight. You know what you're permitted to have. Eat exactly that and not one crumb more. It's your health and your appearance that is important, so when the gravy boat is passed your way, keep it moving.

Just one more tip. Although I have to admit that eating is fun, I've found the best pastime of all is talking. When my mouth is happily occupied going up and down, I find I don't need food. Therefore, it's a good idea to bone up on some good topics of conversation before you attend any social event where food will be served.

SIX

SNACKS—THE WITCHING SNITCHING HOURS

⋧*Introduction*

    And now here's just what you have always wanted—a diet that allows you not only to eat between meals, but virtually recommends that you do so. By dividing the day's calorie intake into three meals plus between-meal snacks, the Special Diet ensures the inclusion of all of the essential nutrients in a reducing diet and assures your appetite of satisfaction at all times.

The nice thing about the unlimited vegetables on the Special Diet is that in addition to truly keeping us from being physically hungry, they also break the habit of snacking on forbidden foods. Much as I may have liked frosting, I was never tempted to put it on my celery. There's also a limit to just how many raw vegetables you can consume. It's possible to eat four or five radishes and stop—have you ever tried that with peanuts?

As with many endeavors, the most important factor is to know yourself. The sound of little feet pattering about in the night doesn't necessarily mean that there are small children in the house; it could mean that there is a compulsive eater dwelling there.

Many's the night I would get up at three o'clock in the morning and find myself in front of the refrigerator nibbling on the cold leftovers from dinner. The leftovers included such unappetizing items as cold French fried potatoes (who else saves cold French fried potatoes but a compulsive eater?) and cold spaghetti.

Forty-two pounds lighter, I can report that I still am a middle-of-the-night prowler. What keeps my figure in line is that there are no dangerous foods lurking there—just a little cherry gelatine maybe, or some skim milk. Definitely nothing to test my willpower.

It takes strength to know your weaknesses. If you are a night eater, especially the kind who gets up in the middle of the night for that midnight snack, it would not be wise to leave the kitchen after dinner without having something ready and waiting in your refrigerator. Something good. As the night progresses and you become more fatigued, your resistance to goodies will be weaker. Don't test this; take my word for it. Or examine the habits that got you where you are right now. You'll see readily that this principle holds. Once that over-powering urge for something to eat takes over, there's no time for cooking. Have your treats waiting in the refrigerator, ready to be devoured.

As you know, a piece of cake doesn't need any preparation—it's ready to be slipped into your mouth (later to dwell on your hip line). Therefore your Special Diet food must be in the same state of readiness. I once spent several minutes at the kitchen sink debating whether or not to make an instant mousse. Once having decided to go ahead, it took no time at all to prepare. Now I automatically boil extra water in the morning and make the instant mousse before washing up the breakfast dishes. When I come home from work and look urgently for "something" satisfying, it is there.

I am a 4-o'clock snacker. I find that having a milk shake at this hour is just not satisfying enough, so I start off with a box of frozen string beans cooked until just heated through so that they will remain crunchy. I toss them with a few shakes of grated American cheese. You may prefer asparagus or broccoli, or a can of mushrooms prepared the same way. This is followed with a bit of mousse or a fruit, and then I have a milk shake. This suits me.

Your hunger may strike at ten at night. Don't wait for it to come over you. Meet it halfway by having something—perhaps the ice cream—ready and waiting for you. Maybe you will want a substantial snack—a three-course one like mine, or more if you feel inventive. You're permitted. Know what your needs are, then shop and cook for them.

I. LIMITED QUANTITY SNACKING

These foods are limited during the day, but may be broken up between meals and snacks, or reserved in toto for snack times:

Skim milk or Buttermilk. Check for your allotted daily allowance. Drink them plain or flavored, in milk shakes or ice cream or custards.

Fruit. Again, check your allotted daily portion.

II. UNLIMITED QUANTITY SNACKING

Remember, it doesn't make any difference if you have already had these at mealtime, or for desserts—you can have them again, and all you want of them.

Unlimited vegetables, cooked or raw. Try raw and chopped (all varieties) with seasoning salts or powders.

Gelatine desserts (dietetic).

Low-calorie soda.

Bouillon. Don't forget—with seasonings, spices and un-limited vegetables, you can make all manner of soups. Pickles (not sweet, unless you make them yourself with artificial sweetener).

When searching for an idea for a snack, review the cookbook, jotting down those foods that would belong either in limited quantity or unlimited quantity.

To me, and perhaps to you, the ability to snack whenever I feel like it is the difference between happiness and misery on a reduction or maintenance diet. There are those who always have been and always will be satisfied with three good meals a day, and nothing in between. But I am not one of them, nor do I expect to be. At last I can stop feeling guilty and desperate about it—I can also recognize my shortcomings.

One of my former neighbors laughed when I tried to talk her into going on the Special Diet. "Heavens, Lois," she exclaimed, "I only eat one meal a day." I started to agree. I had watched her dig into the children's leftover cereal before they even made it down the walk to the school bus, and no matter what hour of the day or night I stopped by, she was always chewing on some-thing. Evidently this was not what she had been referring to as she went on to explain that even though dinner was the only meal she ate, she merely picked at her food. If I am ever able to convince her to try the Special Diet, it will suit her needs to perfection. However, at the moment she is firmly convinced that she is just one of those unfortunates who gains weight by merely smelling food.

There's one thing certain about being overweight—you can't get it off by making excuses or by starving. And even praying may not do you much good. Your method has to be worthy of the results. You must know your weaknesses and learn how to cope with them.

SNACKS—DRINK TYPE— LIMITED

Mint Cooler   (FOUR FRUIT SERVINGS)

>   1 cup water
>   1 tablespoon liquid sugar substitute
>   ½ cup chopped mint leaves
>   ½ cup lemon juice
>   2 cups orange juice
>   1 quart low-calorie ginger ale

Mix all ingredients together.

Vanilla Frosted   (ONE MILK SERVING)

>   8 ounces low-calorie cream soda
>   ⅓ cup dry milk
>   4 ice cubes

Blend all together until ice has been blended in thoroughly.

Hawaiian Company Drink   (FIVE FRUIT SERVINGS)

>   ½ cup lemon juice
>   2½ cups unsweetened pineapple juice
>   ¾ cup lime juice
>   4 teaspoons liquid artificial
>   sweetener
>   1 quart low-calorie ginger ale

Combine juices and sweetener. Divide into ten glasses. Fill glasses with chilled ginger ale.

Coffee Milkshake   (ONE MILK SERVING)

    1 teaspoon instant coffee
    ½ cup liquid skim milk
    ½ teaspoon vanilla
    1 ice cube
    2 packs artificial sweetener
    ¼ cup powdered skim milk

Place all ingredients in blender on low speed until ice has been blended thoroughly.

SNACKS—DRINK TYPE—
UNLIMITED

Lemonade

    2 cups lemon juice
    4 teaspoons grated lemon peel
    16 packs artificial sweetener

Combine all ingredients in glass jar and store in refrigerator. To make lemonade, pour ¼ cup of this mixture into a tall glass. Fill glass with ice cubes and water. Stir.

Any Low-Calorie Soda

SNACKS–DESSERT TYPE–
LIMITED

"Applesauce Candy"   (TWO FRUIT SERVINGS)

> 1 cup dietetic applesauce
> 1 package dietetic cherry gelatine

Boil applesauce. Dissolve gelatine in applesauce and spread in small pan. Cool. Chill. Cut in squares.

Frozen Lemon Custard   (ONE MILK SERVING)

Step 1

> 1 egg yolk
> ¼ teaspoon grated lemon rind
> 3 tablespoons lemon juice
> 1 tablespoon liquid sweetener

Mix all ingredients together.

Step 2

> 1 egg white
> ⅓ cup water
> ⅓ cup dry milk powder

Mix all together. Fold Step 1 ingredients into mixture. Pour into freezing tray. Freeze. (Recipe contains the equivalent of 2 ounces of protein.)

Strawberry Ice Cream
(TWO MILK SERVINGS AND ONE FRUIT SERVING)

8 ounces evaporated skim milk
4 packs artificial sweetener
12 strawberries

Freeze milk to crystal stage in ice cube tray. Chill mixing bowl and beaters. Beat milk with sweetener until the consistency of heavy whipped cream. Add strawberries. Cover and re-freeze.

Dairy Delight
(ONE MILK SERVING AND ONE FRUIT SERVING)

⅓ cup skim milk powder
2 packs artificial sweetener
⅓ cup low-calorie cherry soda
12 whole strawberries

Blend milk powder, sweetener and soda on low speed. Freeze for 30 minutes.

TOO GOOD TO BE TRUE GOODIES—EXTREMELY LIMITED DESSERTS AND SNACKS

The following recipes can be used as dessert or snacks. CAUTION: They are very high in at least one of the limited food categories—they are legal, however, insofar as they do not contain anything from the Taboo list. *Be sure to make proper deductions from meals.*

Frozen Taffy   (TWO MILK SERVINGS)

> *2 eggs, well beaten*
> *1 teaspoon vanilla*
> *½ teaspoon maple extract*
> *⅔ cup skim milk powder*
> *4 packs artificial sweetener*

Combine eggs, extracts, milk and sweetener. Beat well. Freeze. Vary flavoring and sprinkle with cinnamon or nutmeg. (Recipe contains the equivalent of 4 ounces of protein.)

Lemon Cookies   (TWO MILK SERVINGS)

> *⅔ cup skim milk powder*
> *4 egg whites*
> *4 packs artificial sweetener*
> *1 teaspoon grated lemon rind*

Beat egg whites until stiff, fold in powdered skim milk and sweetener and lemon rind. Bake at 325° for 5 minutes, then at 250° for 45 minutes to 1 hour depending on oven. Sprinkle with cinnamon or nutmeg. (Recipe contains the equivalent of 2 ounces of protein.)

Cheese Pie

2 eggs
1 pound farmer cheese
¼ cup buttermilk
16 packs artificial sweetener
1 tablespoon lemon juice
1 teaspoon vanilla

Blend all together. Pour into glass Pyrex dish. Bake at 375° for 15 minutes. Pour Diet Workshop sour cream on top mixed with sweetener and cinnamon and bake 5 minutes more or use strawberry jelly recipe for glaze topping. (Recipe contains the equivalent of 11 ounces of protein.)

Chocolate Pudding   (FOUR MILK SERVINGS)

½ cup water
2 packets unflavored gelatine
1 package chocolate skim milk powder
1 cup boiling water
8 ice cubes

Put cold water in blender and sprinkle gelatine over to soften. Dissolve with hot water and turn blender on "low." Add chocolate skim milk powder and add ice cubes one at a time. Pour into individual serving cups.

Pumpkin Pie
(FOUR LIMITED VEGETABLE SERVINGS AND ONE AND ONE-HALF MILK SERVINGS)

> 1 16-ounce can pumpkin
> 2 packs artificial sweetener
> ½ teaspoon salt
> 1½ cups skim milk
> 1 teaspoon ginger
> ½ teaspoon nutmeg
> ½ teaspoon cinnamon
> 1 egg, well beaten

Mix all ingredients together. Bake at 375° for 1 hour or until knife comes out clean. (Recipe contains the equivalent of 2 ounces of protein.)

Lemon Sponge Cake   (TWO MILK SERVINGS)

> 4 egg whites
> ⅔ cup dry milk powder
> 4 egg yolks
> 1 package dietetic lemon gelatine
> 1 teaspoon vanilla

Beat egg whites stiff. Add remaining ingredients and mix together. Bake in 8 x 6 pan in 350° oven for 12-15 minutes. (Recipe contains the equivalent of 8 ounces of protein.)

No-Bake Cheese Pie

    1½ packets unflavored gelatine
    ½ cup cold water
    2 eggs, separated
    1 tablespoon lemon juice
    1 teaspoon vanilla
    7 packs artificial sweetener
    1 pound cottage cheese
    4 ice cubes

Soften gelatine in cold water. Dissolve over low heat. Place all ingredients except egg whites in blender and blend until smooth. Beat egg whites in mixer until stiff but not dry. Fold cheese mixture into egg whites. Pour into 10-inch plate and refrigerate. To glaze cheese pie, prepare dietetic red gelatine according to package directions. When it starts to set, pour over chilled, set cheese pie. (Recipe contains the equivalent of 12 ounces of protein.)

Chocolate Candy   (FOUR MILK SERVINGS)

    1 package chocolate skim milk powder
    1 teaspoon vanilla
    7 teaspoons water

Mix vanilla with water. Add to chocolate, mixing well. Roll into small balls about 1 inch in diameter. Freeze.

Cheese Wafers   (TWO MILK SERVINGS)

> 4 egg whites
> ⅔ cup skim milk powder
> 4 teaspoons grated cheese
>   Toasted onion flakes (optional)

Beat egg whites until stiff. Fold in powdered milk, cheese and any other seasonings you wish. Drop by teaspoon onto Teflon cookie sheet. Bake at 325° for 5 minutes, then at 250° for 20 minutes. You may have to experiment with your oven to get the right timing for crispy wafers. (Recipe contains the equivalent of 2 ounces of protein.)

SNACKS—DESSERT TYPE— UNLIMITED

Spiced Rhubarb

> 1½ pounds rhubarb
> ½ cup water
> ½ cup vinegar
> 2 teaspoons cinnamon
> ¼ teaspoon powdered cloves
> 4 tablespoons liquid sweetener

Cut rhubarb into 1-inch pieces. Place in large saucepan with other ingredients. Cover and simmer over low heat for 20 to 25 minutes. Chill.

Steamed Rhubarb

1½ pounds rhubarb
1 or 2 tablespoons boiling water
8 packages artificial sweetener

Cut rhubarb into 1-inch pieces. Add to boiling water. Cover pot. Keep on low heat and steam until rhubarb is tender. Add artificial sweetener. Stir and serve hot or chilled.

Any Dietetic Gelatine

Serve plain.
Chill until syrupy. Whip.
Chill until syrupy. Whip with buttermilk.
(Milk must be counted.)
Chill until syrupy. Whip with skim milk powder.
(Milk must be counted.)
Layer different flavors in glasses or mold.
Add dietetic or fresh fruit. (Fruit must be counted.)

SNACKS—MISCELLANEOUS— UNLIMITED

For Sitting and Snacking

Take your favorite raw vegetables—celery, radishes, cucumbers, cauliflower—and cut into chunks. Sprinkle with garlic powder.

Sour Pickles

> 2 to 3 garlic cloves
> 7 to 8 cucumber pickles
> 1 teaspoon pickling spice
>   Salt to taste
> 2 teaspoons vinegar
>   Boiling salt water

Wash half-gallon jar in very hot water. Cut cloves of garlic into small pieces and place half in bottom of jar. Pack washed cucumber pickles into jar. Add spices and vinegar. Pour boiling salt water over pickles. Cover lightly. Keep in warm place until as sour as desired. Chill.

Mushroom "Nuts"

> Drain liquid from can of mushroom buttons.
> Place mushrooms in a 325° oven on a sheet of
> aluminum foil. Bake 1 hour.

Red Cabbage Slaw

> 1 pound raw red cabbage
> 4 red radishes, sliced thin
>   Salt, pepper to taste
> 1 teaspoon vinegar

Grate cabbage. Toss all ingredients together. Chill.

SEVEN

HOW DOES A VACATION FIT INTO YOUR DIET?

VACATION TIME

I have one standard bit of advice for people who are going on vacation while dieting: Don't be a martyr.

It is possible to lose weight while staying at a luxury hotel or going on a cruise, but havoc sets in the week after. Following the first proud weigh-in (and most people make a dash for the scale before they do anything else), all control breaks loose. I have yet to analyze whether this is due to the reward instinct or whether it is because you feel so sorry for yourself because of all the goodies you passed up for "the cause."

So the best advice I can give you is to practice maintenance . . . don't count on returning home with a great weight loss, but try not to come back with a weight gain. Try to remain the same. Be moderate, but if there is something you really want, have it. When you arrive home, go right back on the diet as rigidly as before.

Vacations are fun, but so is being thin. Don't use your diet as an excuse for staying home, but don't use your vacation as an excuse for going "hog wild." Be sensible and watch what you are putting in your mouth. Unless you are aware of what you are eating, you'll find that frequently you can start consuming everything in sight—whether you want it or not. If you feel that you *must* have a rich dessert, by all means order it. But if you can be equally happy with a fresh fruit compote, enjoy that instead.

Incidentally, this is not a drinking man's diet. If on maintenance you wish to have *a* drink, that's fine; but for the period of time you are trying to lose—no alcohol, please. We have reasons to defend our position. First of all, alcohol does have extra calories. In the second place, it's so easy to have a second drink after you have had the first, because alcohol weakens the will—that's one of its attractions. Once you've had the second drink you are apt to throw caution to the winds and say to yourself, "What the heck, I'll go off the diet this one night. So it will take me a week longer to be thin, what difference does it make?" It does make a difference. I believe that weight should come off just as quickly as possible. One shouldn't drag the diet out interminably. Once your taste buds are whetted by foods you haven't tasted for a while, it may be difficult for you to return to the proper plan. Our last reason for avoiding alcohol is because it is an appetite stimulant, and let's face it—that is the last thing a dieter needs, especially at a time when she or he is least likely to find the foods that can be eaten with impunity.

John R. has been on and off more diets than he, or anyone else, can count. His pattern has been to lose 12 or 14 pounds and then rapidly gain them back. John is a salesman. He travels a great deal and entertains clients three or four times a week. The dining presents no great problem as the hotels and restaurants he frequents can readily serve him the seafood, lean meats, salads, vegetables and fruits that are required on the Special Diet. It's the wining that always got John in trouble. He'd be fine for a few weeks—sipping on his low-calorie soda or tomato juice and watching his client put away several scotches. Then the inevitable would happen. Although he had no particular craving for alcohol, he would tire of explaining his reason for not drinking and would become overly sensitive about any remarks that were made pertaining to his having to diet. Then it wasn't long before he was back on the three-martinis-before-lunch routine. It had happened so many times that finally John's doctor issued the warning: "Stop drinking, or else. . . ."

John returned to his diet, but this time he had heart-to-heart chats with the bartenders in his favorite restaurants. Now when he sits down with a client and orders "the usual" for himself, his martini glass arrives with a small pearl onion floating in low-calorie ginger ale. No, he's not trying to fool anyone. Experience has taught John that when his diet becomes a subject of discussion, it causes a feeling of deprivation that soon defeats his weight-reducing program.

So, whether you're on vacation or at home, for the present do your toasting with low-calorie soda. No one need know, or care, what is in your glass. And by following this routine, you will find that you can get high on the compliments that come your way.

EIGHT

WEIGHT CHARTS AND PERSONAL SCORE CARD

WEIGHT CHART

WOMEN

HEIGHT		WEIGHT		
FEET	INCHES	SMALL FRAME	MEDIUM FRAME	LARGE FRAME
4	9	105	114	122
4	10	108	116	124
4	11	110	118	126
5	0	113	121	129
5	1	116	124	132
5	2	120	128	136
5	3	123	132	140
5	4	127	136	144
5	5	130	139	148
5	6	134	142	152
5	7	138	146	156
5	8	142	150	160
5	9	146	154	163
5	10	150	158	166
5	11	154	162	170
6	0	158	166	174

Weight Chart information courtesy of Metropolitan Life Insurance Company.

WEIGHT CHART

MEN

| HEIGHT | | WEIGHT | | |
FEET	INCHES	SMALL FRAME	MEDIUM FRAME	LARGE FRAME
5	0	118	126	134
5	1	121	129	137
5	2	124	132	140
5	3	127	135	143
5	4	131	139	147
5	5	134	142	150
5	6	138	146	154
5	7	142	150	158
5	8	146	154	162
5	9	150	158	166
5	10	154	162	170
5	11	158	166	176
6	0	164	172	182
6	1	170	178	188
6	2	178	184	194
6	3	184	190	200

(Weight and height as ordinarily dressed but without shoes, coat and vest.)

Weight Chart information courtesy of Metropolitan Life Insurance Company.

WEIGHT CHART

TEENAGE GIRLS

HEIGHT		WEIGHT						
FEET	INCHES	YEARS 12	YEARS 13	YEARS 14	YEARS 15	YEARS 16	YEARS 17	YEARS 18
4	2	62						
4	3	65						
4	4	67						
4	5	69	71					
4	6	71	73					
4	7	75	77	78				
4	8	79	81	83				
4	9	82	84	88	92			
4	10	86	88	93	96	101		
4	11	90	92	96	100	103	104	
5	0	95	97	101	105	108	108	111
5	1	100	101	105	108	112	113	116
5	2	105	106	109	113	115	117	118
5	3	110	110	112	116	117	119	120
5	4	114	115	117	119	120	122	123
5	5	118	120	121	122	123	125	126
5	6		124	124	125	128	129	130
5	7		128	130	131	133	133	135
5	8		131	133	135	136	138	138
5	9			135	137	138	140	142

Weight Chart information courtesy of Metropolitan Life Insurance Company.

WEIGHT CHART

TEENAGE BOYS

HEIGHT		WEIGHT						
FEET	INCHES	YEARS 12	YEARS 13	YEARS 14	YEARS 15	YEARS 16	YEARS 17	YEARS 18
4	2	58						
4	3	61						
4	4	64	64					
4	5	68	68					
4	6	71	71	72				
4	7	74	74	74				
4	8	77	78	78	80			
4	9	81	82	83	83			
4	10	85	85	86	87			
4	11	89	89	90	90	90		
5	0	92	93	94	95	96		
5	1	96	97	99	100	103	106	
5	2	101	102	103	104	107	111	116
5	3	106	107	108	110	113	118	123
5	4	109	111	113	115	117	121	126
5	5	114	117	118	120	122	127	131
5	6		119	122	125	128	132	136
5	7		124	128	130	134	136	139
5	8			134	134	137	141	143
5	9			137	139	143	146	149
5	10						151	154

Weight Chart information courtesy of Metropolitan Life Insurance Company.

NAME _____

HEIGHT _____ **GOAL** _____

DATE	WEIGHT	LOSS

SUBJECT INDEX

RECIPE INDEX